# Management of Humility

### Healing people and Companies from arrogance

HILDEMARO INFANTE

©*Gerencia de la humildad.*
*Sanando personas y empresas de la soberbia*
© Hildemaro Infante
Originally published in Spanish in 2017

Cover: Hildemaro Infante
Editorial Coordination: Nelson Cordido
Art editor: Liliana Acosta
English translation: Álvaro Infante Lorenzo
Edition: Daniel Andrés Di Bartolomeo

Ediciones H. Infante & Asociados
More Information:

 Hildemaro Infante

 @hinfantei

 www.hinfante.com

 http://www.youtube.com/user/h012402

All rights reserved. The total or partial reproduction of this work is not allowed, nor its incorporation to a computer-based system, or its transmission in any way, electrical, mechanical, photocopy, recording or others, without the previous authorization in writing from the beholders of the copyright. The infraction of these rights can constitute a crime against intellectual property.

ISBN-10: 1718859384
ISBN-13: 9781718859388

# MANAGEMENT OF HUMILITY

 The symbol of this portrait belongs to the Ashanti ethnic group from Ghana. With horns of a ram representing the force of humbleness in all aspects of our lives, to acquire knowledge and eradicate arrogance.

HILDEMARO INFANTE

DEDICATION

*To my wife María del Mar and my sons Victoria, Javier and Alvaro, my motivation and joy.*

*In the memory of my parents, Hildemaro and Eugenia who are always leading my steps.*

# INTRODUCTION

*Alejandro Serrano Caldera*[1]

Hildemaro Infante's book Managing Humility. Healing people and companies from arrogance, is a reflection that leads people to rethink about the values and principles that constitute the essential nature, such as the identity of a person, a company or even society, on its particular and internal condition, but also in the relation that involves them all, the interaction it produces and influences its individual and collective characterization.

---

[1] Jurist, philosopher and writer from Nicaragua. Visiting professor in Universities of Europe, United States and Latin America. Rector of the Universidad Nacional Autónoma de Nicaragua, UNAN-Managua, 1990-94. President of the council of national universities, CNU, 1990-94 y President of the Superior universitary council of Central America universities. (CSUCA) 1993-1994. Member of the UN Committee of Human Rights.
Nicaragua´s Ambassador to France from 1979-85, Ambassador of Nicaragua to the UN. 88-90. President of the Supreme Justice Court of Managua, Nicaragua 1985-1988.
Number Member of the Academia Nigaragüense de la Lengua. Has published over 20 books in subjects as Philosophy, Law and Political science.

Humility is assumed as an essential value that defines the subject that practices it and identifies the company in which the subject works and changes the predominant concept that everyone has about this value and its functioning in the business world.

Companies are not a battlefield between the elements of capital and workforce, but the center of convergence and shared interests that come from several points and places. This is the reason why humility should be assumed with an ethical purpose, it's the common wellbeing of companies and society. From this point of view the concept of humility should be understood as an essential finality of new leadership, in which, to be honest should as Hildemaro Infante says, have a "high dose of humility and modesty" and also "not live from past accomplishments and to consider the future as an objective", because "leadership can't be bought or imposed, it surges from the inner-self of each person"

Humility is the balance between knowledge, experiences and human quality "With humility, an authentic leader has the goal of doing good to its company and society"

It is also necessary to establish the relationship between political order, governability, leadership and humility, just as the book suggests referring to the line that Samuel Huntington describes in his work "The political order in changing societies"

It is this way that Hildemaro Infante develops the concept of humility as an expression of the fundamental values of a person, company and society; it is, from his axiological qualification that treats different subjects starting from the bare concept of humility and the sense it assumes in businesses; leadership; communication that forces you to know how to listen to your interlocutor; personal service and empathy; to then, based in confidence establish a relation between the professional, ethic and happiness

I consider that Hildemaro Infante's book, through the different aspects it covers, reaffirms three fundamental subjects: Values, ethic and Human Rights.

Values define the subject. The virtue, justice, kindness and in this case, humility, are values that qualify the person. Ethic is formed by ethos, that is precisely the system of values and principles that constitutes it. In its larger sense, ethic is the adequacy of action to ends "a knowledge of morals values", as José Ferrater Mora defines it; "A group of behaviour rules and ways to live life to make the man realize the value of the good" as Eduardo García Maynez says, Aristotle in its Ethics to Nicomaco says "the good of each activity is the end that it leans to. All the acts of men chase a determined finality and in its consecution finds its own good"

Human rights are constituted by the convergence of this values and principles, in this sense they're the moral philosophy of our time and as such, they lay in an integral ethic according to each problem and contradiction that is debated in our days. Therefore, they're the bases of universal contemporary humanism.

Humility is a condition of a person that allows them to connect these categories, because through them the subject can perceive and practice them in his own nature and with other people. From this point the "ethos" conforms ethics as a system of practical rules that affects the behavior of the collective and the individual and holds the fundamental rights of the human being.

In this sense, humility, as it comes framed in the book we're commenting, isn't a diminution of the valuation of the subject, or a devaluation of the self-esteem, but the opening and tolerance to listen and attend different - and even opposed - points of view, to accept other people's arguments if they're capable of convincing you, or keeping your own if they reaffirm the conviction and criterion that holds them.

We hope that the valuable message that is contained in this book and the input that it has given to this subject, can contribute to encourage tolerance and critical thinking.

HILDEMARO INFANTE

# PREFACE

**V**alues are learned at home. Parents that were implied in raising children never gave lessons on how to do it, they transmitted formation modeled on their daily behavior and giving a good example to their children. This way they made sure that the people who surrounded them internalized their principles, turning them into several regulators of their conduct needed to orient in a positive way their aspirations, contributing these way to make our society better.

The values can be defined according to their nature:

- **Personal values (human):** they're learned at home, mostly from the parents and are derived from the premises that allow social acceptance and impulse the human being in its progress and continuous advance.

- **Collective values:** they're principles that generate common actions from individuals that belong to a certain group.

- **Cultural values:** They're the support of a country's identity, region or town and highlights their traditions.

In the category of human values, humbleness has a starring role for being, aside from a value, an essential competence that every human being should have and practice; their possibilities to achieve goals, prosperity, personal and professional completeness are dependent upon this. When someone sets up a goal and isn't humble enough to understand that they don't know everything and that they'll eventually need help, they can suffer through the road, therefore their chances to succeed and accomplish their goals will be limited from the start.

In the corporate world there are well known cases of businesses that experiment a lot of clients leaving them for the bad service they received, but also because they felt like no one was listening nor attending their needs.

If companies do not practice humbleness they lose sight of what's important. Being the leader of the market has nothing to do with superiority, but instead it is related to serving, listening and understanding other people's needs.

One of the key elements that has a lot of influence in the current crisis of human values at companies, is the lack of humility that people usually have. The competitive environment allows you to reinvent yourself, attending to the trends of the market. Humility brings you the strength needed to recognize mistakes and to prioritize the client's needs, apply correctives that are needed to consolidate responsible leaders, at the same time that you protect the reputation and brand of the company.

Falling and rising up with dignity is an essential part of the circle of life of every entrepreneur, professional and human being. People should not be defined by the amount of goods they have, the power the hold above others, the prestige or popularity, but by what they are and the aspects of their conduct that define them.

Humility is the competence that allows human beings, when they talk about themselves, to refer to what they are and not to what they have. A human being who is humble listens and understands other people's points of view even if they do not agree with them. A word pronounced with humbleness means more than a thousand words said with arrogance.

These pages have the goal of providing a simple guide to know the conducts that are associated with humbleness as a value and human competence, with the objective of practicing it, making easier the continuous learning, the development of vocation to serve and to be comprehensive professionals, who identify the road to dreams and the possibilities of accomplishing these, making a positive impact in our daily behavior and translating to practice what we say and think.

**Who's the best farmer?**

The one who knows with all the details the qualities of terrains, weathers, seeds and plants. The one who knows which are the best methods and instruments to work with. The one who identifies means to make the land produce with the least costs, in prime quantities and time. The best farmer is the one who has the most knowledge about the practice of his occupation.

Attending to this approach, the focus of this content is to give several workplace experiences in very diverse roles.

- **Employee and manager:** Occupied managing positions in leading companies of the retail, services and manufacturing sectors.

- **Management consultant:** Executing several projects in Central America, Equator, Colombia and Venezuela. In the areas of strategic planning, assessment of companies, analysis of processes, keys of value to the retail sector, developing happy workplace environments, selecting talent, forming high performance teams and quality labor relations.

- **Teacher:** Imparting training, for more than twelve years in graduate programs in the subjects of: Purchases, retail basis, market metrics and high performance teams.

- **Writer:** Author of the book "Pyramid of labour happiness" where we propose that we spend more time working than anywhere else in our adult lives, so we must achieve happiness and completeness in our workplace, because when you love what you do, the chances of being happy in your personal life rise a lot.

All of these experiences have been put to the service of this content, with the goal of providing the reader with reality, possibilities of practical application, enjoyment and reflection about how the advantages of humbleness as a value and competence, that allows us to recognize the limits of capacities, to have a clear fortitude, manage success in a quiet way, to strengthen other people, to listen to everyone, and last but definitely not least important, always staying alert learning from everything and everyone.

The author

# 1. Humility

**M**any times we hear a word or a concept and we can handle it in an emotional way. A word that triggers emotions and repeats itself without analyzing what we are saying. We repeat the word supposing it has the same meaning to everyone. Concepts and words have different meanings, depending on everyone's interpretation of it. This is the reason why we need to ask ourselves about the origins of words.

## Meaning of humility

Going deeper into the meaning of the word humility. Etymology says that humility comes from the word humus, those natural fertilizers that make nature grow. What is essential to you in your life, family, work or hobbies? Every single person has something that they consider important, their true essence. The rest is superficial but it is hard to identify and recognize that.

When people surround themselves with superficial things and their objective isn't to enjoy them but just to have them, are they clear about the things that have value in their lives ? Material things do not last with time, that's undeniable and in no way can anyone keep a person apart from their good memories and times of enjoyment. Is it best to invest in memories than in luxury items? How do we avoid being superficial? How do we turn back to the essence? Humility has the answers to those questions.

## The concept of humility

Humility is an inherent concept to human beings; it is described in the world's most known management book: The Bible, where it's defined as loving others without being weak.

*Do nothing out of selfish ambition or vain conceit. Rather, in humility value others above yourselves*

Philippians 2:3.

When you're humble you can handle injustices, answering with smart and self-possession, without being dominated by anger. With humility you do not need revenge, tearing apart frustrations and anger. When you're humble you can learn from people questioning you without adopting a defensive attitude, with the capacity of recognizing if it's well deserved or not. Likewise, mistakes and failures are taken with consciousness and always leave lessons.

Frequently, when someone is trying to describe a high-ranking executive they picture a cold, non-sensitive, determined, cruel and vicious person, with a whole line of teeth ready to devour its next victim. Nonetheless, reality is that each day more professionals consider humility as a key value of a good leader, we need to learn to be humble as Nitin Noria, dean of Harvard Business School says.

When the magazine Bloomberg Businessweek asked him: What is the thing that future company leaders should now? His answer was clear: "Humility". Maybe his answer wasn't methodical or academic, but it is clear that it has a high dose of humanity.

Company leaders often have an excess of confidence and an exaggerated sense of strength of character. (...)
Developing character is a process of life similar to the development of knowledge (...) business schools should teach people not to fall in arrogance.

Humility is the meaning of leadership to the deans of the most influential business schools in the world.

The behavior of people in marketing strategies of social network celebrates arrogance, presumption and unmeasured attention to themselves. Human beings set aside their essence and become more and more competitive, not to satisfy their needs but their desire of attention, obsessed for superficial things and each time more selfish. Pride is focused on what others think and say in a appearance, while humility is focused only in realities and what the person thinks of himself.

The instinctive rejection of many executives to the word humility comes from a fundamental misunderstanding with the concept. Mainly because it is associated with poverty and low self-esteem, when in reality humility is the competence of leadership that leads to better teamwork, listening to the client and partners, the attention to external dynamics and the possibility of continuous learning.

Many executives show an excessive confidence in their force of character, they feel safe to deal with any problem avoiding the confrontation of opinions with others. When a leader has the only point of view they take the risk of leaving aside the overview of problems and in this way all the decisions will be taken hierarchically, without considering the elements that surround it and the business environment. This attitude sets us apart from the world and imposes the illusion of being invincible and perfect, which is the prelude to failure.

In a study done by Martin Seligman, founder of the Positive Psychology and author of Character strengths and virtues, humility characterizes itself this way:

- A deep consciousness about abilities.
- The ability to recognize mistakes, shortcomings and limits.
- The opening to new ideas, contradicting suggestions about what you think.
- An approach not exclusive to oneself.
- The virtue of appreciating others contribution

Humble people do not believe that goals are achieved by luck, but that they should chase those goals on the same conditions as others. This approach leads them to have a perspective of the world less contaminated by prejudice, inviting them to be tolerant with others and not to be slaves of their own beliefs, which does not mean that we should be permissive, but assertive and to fight with generosity for what we believe in respecting yourself and others. Humility, in fact, helps to reinforce and repair relationships, and to build stronger bonds between people.

## Humility as a value

There is no doubt that values are the regulators of behavior learnt at home. When you analyze humility as a value, you put in evidence that it has nothing to do with poverty, or with being submissive and obeying others, but that it's closely related to listening and learning from others, respecting and collaborating in everything possible. It is ignoring arrogance and recognizing the physique, intellectual and emotional capabilities of others.

Humility is a sign of grandeur that allows people to be worth of trust, flexible and adaptable. A humble person can work and achieve an optimum performance in distinct environments, applying coherence of thought with acting, because in order to demand rights you should first get your duty done.

> **Humility = Personal strength**

Humbleness is being realistic, knowing and viewing ourselves as what are. Only in this way we can take advantage of what we have to achieve the maximum personal and work performance. Realizing the main aspects of our character and ourselves, like abilities that we have not been taking advantage of or aptitudes that we need to develop in a more in deep way, we must accept those and take the challenge of competing against ourselves, assuming that we have the control and that we can reinvent ourselves to be better.

## Humility as a competence

The model of competences is used in the work environment and is defined as knowing what to do in the context of work. It is the combination of knowledges, capacities and behaviors that can be used in our professional lives and lead to better results in a certain environment.

When we put in practice humility at work we can accept that we don't know everything, we'll need guidance and as any human being we can be corrected and led, thanking it as an aid to be better at what we do.

## ¿How do you put in practice the competence of humility?

A manager of human resources summoned two collaborators to know details about the delay of a certain job that was assigned to them. One of the subordinates, far from recognizing non-fulfillment justified himself without giving any real arguments, and even blamed others for his behavior. The other member of the team recognized that he had planned his time poorly, which caused the delay. In this situations certain doubts come up, such as:

- ¿Who acted better?
- ¿Which one of the two is more trustworthy?

Humility is the light at the end of the tunnel. In the middle of this tunnel you can look behind and go back to the darkness of pride. Instead, if you look to the front you'll see the hope of recognizing mistakes shining, bringing you the opportunity to start again and to transmit calmness in our jobs, companies and lives.

In a session to Mexican entrepreneurs, Carlos Llano, a great academic of the business world, asked the audience what would be their reaction to a complicated employee. One replied: "Firing him". Immediately, Carlos Llano, screaming, told the businessman to leave the room. Didn't you listen? Please leave now! Then, after expelling him, he asked the rest what was their opinion about how he had acted. It must have felt bad, right? This anecdote represents in a graphic way the relation between leadership and humility.

Humility implies not feeling superior to others, but not inferior either. It is expected that you'll serve the company and the community that you live in well, sharing knowledge and experiences to help others, with the goal of aiding them to develop their full potential.

When difficult situations happen at companies, two alternatives are normally presented: Denying or recognizing: The first is centered in the love we have for ourselves, while the second allows us to put ourselves in someone else's shoes. Many of the scandals in the corporate sector are originated by the lack of humility of their executives. This shortage prevented them from correcting in time a little mistake, and this continuity transitioned into an endemic disease, where pride generated direct consequences to them, workers, the company, their brands and their clients.

Leading a company not only demands being careful to the present, but also to act in a correct way to consolidate and help grow the reputation of the organization. The essence of leadership to build a solid organizational future has a backing in humility, because it brings the clients closer and allows them to recognize their actual and future needs, generating relations supported by trust.

Among the attitudes that a manager should have, we can highlight knowing where the company is at, defining where it should go and how to lead themselves and others to that point. Besides these qualities that make easier the management of directors and managers, they must also understand the technical processes that are as relevant as the people working on them. The capacity of integrating multiple things, simplifying the complex, and keeping organizational cohesion are skills that every manager should have.

In moments of crisis, quite frequent in businesses, the leader must be responsible for his acts. Next to the relevance that motivates him to achieve high grounds, he should be a model to form the personnel that is working with him and to develop collaborators that are on the same page as him with his goals.

In conclusion, humility transforms itself into a reliable competence for the construction of leadership of a company that, like the monetary, intellectual and social capital, constitutes a background that allows the company to consolidate itself and grow, and by doing that generates more profitability to the shareholders.

## ¿What is a competence at work?

According to Spencer and Spencer a competency is defined as:

…An underlying characteristic of an individual that is casually related to a criterion referenced as effective or a superior performance in a certain job or situation.

(Spencer y Spencer,1993)

Each day, companies invest more time in taking decisions related to their collaborators: Recruiting, withdrawal, capacitation and development, among others. Being able to carry on the strategy of a business depends directly on the quality, speed and success of those decisions. From a general perspective, the model of management by competences has proven to be a reliable method to predict success or failure of a collaborator working at a certain position in a company.

The model of competences translates knowledge, abilities, and motives from people into observable and repeatable conducts, which can be easily identified and modeled through the management of talent. The competences determine the conducts that are capable of generating results to the company, in the performance of a certain role or in other organizational situations.

## Development of the competency model

Putting in practice the competency model is the result of a

professional and specialized management, sustained in the analysis of the organization, work and people. This model has as an objective to design profiles of success to key jobs that are compatible with the goals of the organization. Its creation demands to have a clear objective, besides explaining how the evolutionary cycle of talent is aligned with the organizational strategy and the results of the business.

One of the main documents that generates this job is the dictionary of competences, where they are mentioned and registered in an ordered way to intervene in certain affairs.

When you analyze most of the dictionaries of competences from the majority of companies, you can easily tell that they don't contain the competence of humility as one of the main conducts to succeed in their workplace. So the departments in charge of picking staff do not have any kind of proof or dynamic that can measure the presence and possibility of putting it to practice. This shortage brings as a consequence that the very own leaders of the company are referents of disloyalty and that areas of management on their behalf work isolated and not as high-performance team representing models of conduct and management, which is wrong and harmful to the whole organization.

## Types of competences

Depending on their application competences can be:

- Competences for the superior performance with means of selection and development.
- Competences in a changing environment, surroundings or the organization itself. Processes of innovation, restructuring, among others.
- Competences to work in self-leading teams or high performance teams.
- Competences for the management of projects.

## How can we incorporate humility to the business model of competences

Humility is connected with consciousness of what we are with our strengths and it brings us the opportunity to grow as human beings by developing a barrier that makes us realize that we are not superior to others and to act accordingly. It is also about accepting that we are not perfect, that we are human, that we make mistakes and we can learn from them. Absence of humility is defined as pride, self-importance or arrogance. Being humble is allowing others to do and to be, with humbleness so we can recognize other people's merits.

## What are the conducts associated with humbleness?

The conducts that are the most recognizable as acts of humility and which allow us to put it into practice as workplace competences are:

- Asking others for their opinion on different matters. Appreciating the most capable people in a certain subject and asking them for help when it's needed.
- Not insisting about accomplishments.
- Admitting lack of knowledge in a subject when we do not understand it.
- Losing the fear of committing mistakes, recognizing what you do wrong and correcting it.
- Not comparing yourself to others or comparing them unnecessarily.
- Giving credit to the true authors of an idea.
- Recognizing that there are always more things to learn.
- Sharing knowledge.
- When you succeed, you should put yourself back in the place you were before accomplishing this success so you do not lose perspective, and also you need to be grateful and not to brag about your accomplishments
- Be willing to listen to others in conversations without prejudices about the transmitter of an idea.

One of the main backings of this competence is having clear that there is no difference between human beings. Nobody is superior to anyone. Everyone has their own value and can be capable of contributing in their own way.

## Who's the responsible of putting humility into practice?

A certain enterprise was bringing their customers a poor service and its collaborators were very arrogant. This conduct was modeled from the directive and was the cause of the poor performance the company was having. Their sales decreased and they almost went broke. Some blamed economic factors, others the luxuries of the executives. Nobody wanted to be the main character of change in the company, assuming their responsibility nor apply the competence of humility.

The shareholders, tired from the labor and human degradation, decided to put at the entrance of the organization a sign that announced the closure of the company because of the death of the collaborator that limited it and prevented it from reaching its potential. The billboard informed that the worker would be unveiled in one of the many conference rooms. Everyone was shocked and very curious, so they went there to see who the worker was. The surprise was very big when they entered the room and saw it full of mirrors that pointed at them all.

> **Putting in practice humility in work and in life depends of each human being**

The technocrats are those persons that are willing to do whatever they have to in order to achieve optimum results, without caring about the consequences that this has in people. A lot of technique and little humanity. Customer service has "mechanized" itself. It is a positive thing that the companies have their own internal processes, but when we subtract our own human quality it is quite complicated to make the client feel cared and respected. Big changes at customer service areas are sustained in fortifying humility in the collaborators. When a client is received with respect and cordiality we are accommodating the terrain to his satisfaction. Technique, experience and knowledge are important factors and always necessary but they always have to be applied towards fulfilling the needs of the client.

> **The success of an organization and a human being = Human quality + technical skills**

## Humility and businesses

One of the first writers that explained the humility in business was the Catholic priest Jaimes Balmes, author of the book "El criterio". The work of the Spanish author has a whole chapter dedicated to humility and its relation with businesses and in this section he details the benefits of the practical application of this value.

- Thanks to humility we know the limit to our strengths. A cold and objective analysis allows us to acknowledge our flaw, which isn't an easy thing to do, and, by then, are permanent obstacles to the progress of what we undertake.

- When a humble attitude is adopted on a daily basis we ask others for their opinion and help. When we apply the benchmarking in a business, we recognize that there are others who are better than us at what we do. There are companies that do not use this technique, not because they don't know it, but because they are hesitant to accept that there are optimal methods to do things and things that you can learn from. Also, Balmes does a lot of emphasis in receiving and listening to people in all levels. Sometimes, the better practices are in the hands of the collaborators located in the base of the pyramid, who in many cases are not taken in consideration accordingly.

- Humility does not put us down, but quite the opposite, it allows us to grow and outdo ourselves. Only if we know what we need to improve we can pretend to be more. Humility acts as a map for the manager to identify his own improper behaviors and to rectify them. It reminds us that we are not superior than our competition and that we need to have the provision to learn from others and the consciousness of being susceptible to improvements.

According to Balmes humility is:

*Humility is the truth, but applied to the knowledge of what we are... humility doesn't let us believe that we have reached the peak in any way, or blind us to the point that we don't see the long way that we need to travel and the advantage that others have over us (...) Humility is a virtue of sum utility in practice, even in mundane things.*

Entrepreneurs can't ignore this principle if they want to consolidate and build a business.

In the last twenty years, a generation of entrepreneurs has managed to achieve success in different business models. Names such as Steve Jobs and Arianna Huffington, among others, have developed a prestige sustained in their own way to visualize opportunities, capitalize them and consolidate successful businesses.

In today's world, where worshipping leaders and those who perform it are each time more evident, a question arises. What place does humility have in the success of businesses? The answer is very simple; it is an essential and necessary element. A study done by the University of Washington Foster School of Business, pointed that the most humble people are more effective leaders, and that they also have high odds of succeeding in their individual management and as the members of a team.

The leaders that are humble are aware of both their strengths and weaknesses, and because of this they know how to recognize the opportunities to improve, because they feel confident about themselves. They do not need vanity; they have an open mind and are integrated easily to the work teams, without being submissive.

Jim Collins, the prestigious guru, quoted and read in the world of management, has studied for years the behavior of companies, analyzing from the most little initiatives to big multinational enterprises. His books have sold over three million copies and have been translated to 35 languages. In them, the author affirms that the true differentiating factor of a great leadership doesn't come from the personality but from humility.

In his book "Why some companies make the lead… and Others don't", Collins establishes the following levels of leadership:

**LEVEL 5**: EXECUTIVE
Builds enduring greatness through a paradoxical combination of personal humility plus professional will

**LEVEL 4**: EFFECTIVE LEADER
Catalyzes commitment to and vigorous pursuit of a clear and compelling vision; stimulates the group to high performance standards

**LEVEL 3**: COMPETENT MANAGER
Organizes people and resources toward the effective and efficient pursuit of predetermined objectives

**LEVEL 2**: CONTRIBUTING TEAM MEMBER
Contributes to the achievement of group objectives; Works effectively with others in a group setting

**LEVEL 1**: HIGHLY CAPABLE INDIVIDUAL
Makes productive contributions through talent, knowledge, skill, and good work habits

HARDVARD BUSINESS REVIEW

Jim Collins defines the superlative level of leadership in the top of the pyramid and classifies it with number 5, illustrating it with a business case that reinforces the presence of humility as a distinctive feature in leaders capable of leading a company to having great results. In 1971, a man whose appearance was very normal called Darwin E. Smith became the managing director of Kimberly-Clark, an old company from the paper industry whose shares had dropped 36% during the previous twenty years. This executive generated a marvelous change, transforming Kimberly-Clark in the leading company in the global paper market. The company overcame all its rivals: Scott Paper and Procter & Gamble. Likewise, its profitability surpassed renowned companies like Coca-Cola, 3M and General Electric.

## How did he do it?

When he became managing director, Darwin E. Smith and his team concluded that the main business of the company, the traditional colored toilet paper, wasn't oriented to a need of the market, so the company was condemned to mediocrity, which lead to its shares dropping more and more every year. The company's finances weren't positive and neither was its competitiveness. Kimberly Clark was obligated to search and find excellence or disappear. Smith announced the resolution of selling the mills that produced the paper and transition to mass consumption paper, investing in companies like Huggies and Kleenex. The press qualified the movement as not smart, in Wall Street the shares dropped their value. In these circumstances Smith did not show signs of weakness. Twenty five years later, Kimberly-Clark owned Scott Paper, and also overtook Procter & Gamble in six of eight categories in the products that were derivatives of paper, in which both companies competed.

Darwin Smith is the classic model of a "Level 5 leader" (an individual who combines personal humility with an intense professional will) Leaders of this kind are the common factor in the extraordinary enterprises studied by Collins. All of them were characterized for being humble individuals who showed a great determination for doing what was needed to make their organization outstanding.

> **Humility becomes the most "elegant" trait in success and is essential in businesses**

# 2. Business Cases

## Humility makes you grow: Johnson & Johnson and Tylenol

In 1982 the company withdrew from the shells of all the stores and supermarkets 31 million of bottles of Tylenol, after eight people died from consuming the poisoned caps with cyanide. The reason or who did it was never known.

The withdrawal cost US$ 240 millions to J&J and cut utilities by almost 50% due to the decline in sales. The situation did not begin in J&J, but the company detached itself from pride and took the most appropriate decision to values and acted before concluding the investigation, withdrawing the product from the market and redesigning the packages so in the future nobody could manipulate them this way.

After one year from the moment that the incident happened, the sales recovered and the brand Tylenol consolidated itself, winning credibility, at the same time that the company gained a huge ethical prestige.

**What happens when a company loses its humbleness?**

**Not recognizing a mistake in time.**

**The fake apple juice of Beech nut Co.**

The company involved in this case, by the moment that the scandal happened was the second most productive in food for babies, with a 15% market share. Bought in 1979 by Nestlé, to recover its prestige it named Niels Hoyvald CEO in 1981. He was a well know executive with a trajectory. In June of 1982 he faced the solid evidence that, since 1977, the company had been commercializing apple juice for babies produced from extracts that did not contain apples; these were acquired because of the low prices.

The Vice-president of the company, John Lavery, did not give a lot of importance to the report that denounced the presence of corn syrup in the juice, as well as other references of the doubtful reputation of the prime material supplier. In this case, a private investigator from the Processed Apple Institute discovered that this provider (Universal Juice Co.) was only producing sugared water and informed Lavery and other executives, inviting them to join a trial against the supplier.

A group of executives pushed to change the supplier and to withdraw the juice from the market. Hoyveld doubted, because he considered that, even if the juice was fake, it wasn't harmful and its flavor was similar to apple and he had a commitment with his superiors from Nestlé in Switzerland to obtain a benefit of US$ 7 millions in that year.

Changing suppliers meant to pay an aggregate of US$ 750,000 per year, and also the withdrawal would cost US$ 3,500,000, leading the company to bankruptcy, with its closure as a direct consequence. Before the state investigations continued and could withdraw from the market the stock of juice, the company launched an aggressive campaign of sales (half-price) outside the US: Puerto Rico and Dominican Republic.

Until March 1983 they kept commercializing their so-called apple juice. When they were ordered to withdraw the product and destroy it there only were 20,000 boxes. In 1988 Hoyvald and Lavery were judged and convicted for the charges of consumer fraud and both received a prison sentence of a year and a fine of US$ 100,000 for each of them. Previously the company Beech-Nut had reached an arrangement related to the charges through the payment of a US$ 2,000,000 fine.

They also agreed to a negotiation of US$ 7,500,000 for the actions initiated by the consumers. Nestle maintained Hoyvald and Lavery in their payroll and took care of their legal expenses for several millions. The judge rejected the motion from Joyvald's attorney that requested to exempt him from prison and having him on trial with the requirement of giving conferences to business students, to deter them from committing his mistakes.

## The questions arise

Which was the best deal for the company? Being humble, acknowledging its mistake and assuming the consequences, or filling itself of pride, hiding it and harming the reputation of its directives, the company, and creating the worst liability for a brand, such as the distrust of its clients? The correct answer does not require much explanation. Upon seeing the outcome of the acts we can conclude with the following equation:

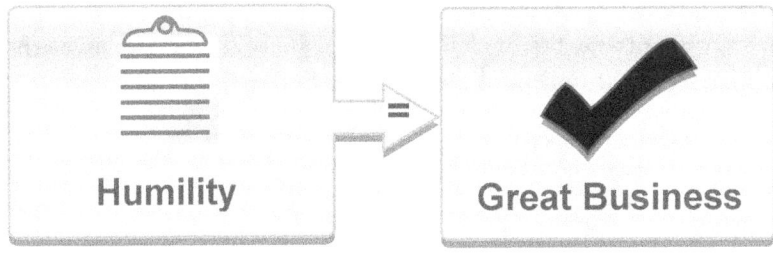

## The pride of the leader, the company that took over the market just to lose it:

Portable music was born with the dream of moving a radio of transistors to any place. In the beginning the equipment was too heavy, hard to move and they had the quality of being portable just because they functioned with batteries. Sony did not invent the transistor radio, but they redesigned it so it was more portable. The portable radio of Sony started to generate positive results and they understood that, if they wanted to continue innovating and fabricating attractive products to their clients, making them more portable was the way to do it.

With the innovation that the cassette represented, the company started fabricating devices that reproduced them. They were very big recorders that were taken from one place to another, in the same way as the radio. The Times magazine talked in an article about the origins of the Walkman the beginning of a revolution to the music playing devices. One of the main executives and founders of Sony, Akio Morita, carried a Sony music player in his business trips, and one day, he got off the plane with the idea of making portable music a private experience. He kept the idea in his head and took it to his engineering team and this way the first original Sony idea was born: On July 1st 1979 the company showed the walkman to the world.

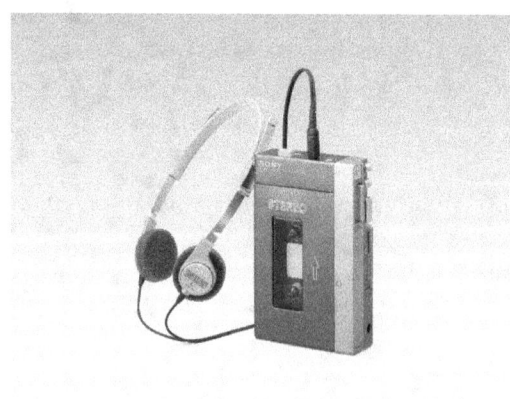

Sony Walkman 1979

As the best inventions, the product mixed a lot of ideas: The cassette, the headphones and portability. This equipment was presented on a blue device, with big buttons. Sony affirmed that they would be commercializing 5,000 devices in Japan after the launching, but in reality this number was multiplied by 10. It was the first time in history that everyone could be walking in the street listening to their own music without interrupting or bothering others.

Other companies such as Aiwa and Philips started to copy the product, but Sony was playing in a better position. The company incorporated new features to its device: Radio, the button they made allowed you to change the basses (called Bass Boost) and a rewinder for the cassette. They even managed to launch to the market a Walkman that used Solar Energy.

The eighties were the years of the Walkman. The device invaded every market in the world, including the American one. Sony started to grow rapidly and started buying American companies.

Then the nineties came and the Compact discs (CDs for short) started to replace the vinyl ones. They were cheaper, easier to produce, and with time the music players became much cheaper. Sony and Phillips allied to develop the first Discman. In the same way and with the same success of the Walkman, this technology ruled the market. We all had a Discman or a Walkman in our hands. The sales of CDs took over without precedents, something that Sony celebrated because they were the owners of one of the most important music producers.

## Sony Discman 1992

With the change of century we saw the Apple proposal. The MP3 music players, among with the digital platform, transformed the music world in a radical way; they offered more benefits to the users for lower prices. On October 23$^{rd}$, 2001, Steve Jobs showed the iPod to the world, and again the music industry changed forever. The iPod not only replaced the Walkman and the Discman, but made the users change their mentality.

The physical discs lost their importance, because the MP3 music files could be downloaded from the web in different platforms. The offered devices for the new format of music expanded the storage capacity, and also had a better, more portable design.

Sony, from its leadership position, in this situation, did not listen to the market and reacted commercializing products that, beyond their creativity and presentations (such as the Mini Disc) proved that they weren't the appropriate ones to cover the needs and the new expectations of their clients because they cost more and were less efficient. In the end, their lack of humility to understand the desires and needs of their clients made them lose money and markets. Their brand, after being positioned among the consumers as a synonymous of top technology, began to be a brand that no longer represented the first choice at the moment of acquiring electronic products.

*Minidisk Model Sony 2002*

Having leaders with egos of huge proportions is negative for companies, because they are the ones contributing to the consequent downfall, continuous mediocrity and their disappearance. The true leadership has a high dose of humility and modesty. A humble leader should act in a balanced way, without incurring in excesses and must take advantage of all the good potential that he has to work well with his collaborators and clients. The humble leader is characterized by his simplicity and asks for help when he requires it. Humility is:

- Never forgetting who we are and where we came from.
- Practicing modesty and not allowing public adulation.
- Establishing rules that regulate, and not making charisma the only criterion.
- Channeling ambitions to their team and the organization, not to themselves.
- Choosing a successor to achieve more success in the next generation.
- Not living from past goals and considering the future as an objective.
- Assigning the success to his collaborators and the commitment of the work team.

In the virtual world of today, known for the communication, information, social networks and CRM, it's harder that these kinds of situations happen because the consumer has more power to decide. However, in the moment that a company stops listening to its clients and loses its humbleness, it starts to shatter because the user stops being the center of the business and its substituted by the pride and ego of its leaders. Listening to the market also means that you should also listen to your clients, what does your client say? What is the client not telling you? Because you also need to interpret his silences to understand what he is asking for and for what things he needs that. Many times people try to think with the client, putting themselves in the client's place and to achieve that we need to manage everything in our lives with humbleness.

## 3. Leadership And Humility

Leadership isn't bought or imposed, it emerges from the inside of each person, although we have to recognize that in today's world it depends a lot on the media exposure that the person has and the kind of megaphone he has to tell his story. A real leader must be consistent and represent substantial values putting them into practice. It isn't improvised; nowadays, organizations should recruit and hire the people who are talented enough and that share their personal values with the company, in particular the ones referred to respect, consideration and, of course, humility, aside from guaranteeing an adequate balance between knowledges, experiences and wealth of their human qualities. This operation translates in a great advantage to companies; transforming them into seedbeds to future leaders at the time they institute a brand of leadership with their own identity, which allows the collaborators to direct their professional trajectory.

> **With humbleness, the true leader has as a goal the common well of the company and society**

### Should a businessman or a politician be humble?

With certain frequency we see politicians put their faces as a reflection of the state's work, as if they were the Government. Similarly we observe the behavior of many business leaders among ethic decisions, where they put their earning before the interests of the clients. We don't have to make polls to conclude that humbleness, in most of the cases, isn't a priority between those who have the responsibility to lead institutions of contemporary society.

It is wrong to generalize, even though it is a reality that most of the political, entrepreneurial and social leaders, aren't prominent because they put into practice the aptitude of humbleness. Many develop and try to consolidate their leadership encouraging the worship to their own self, without paying attention to the magnificent flow of knowledge that the culture of values brings to the table. Among all, the most simple one, which is home formation, allows people to consolidate humility as an essential aptitude to build men of success in life and professionally.

The humble leader is the most appreciated and efficient. The capacity of recognizing his own mistakes, highlighting the potential of his subordinates and providing a good example as a backing of his leadership is the behavior that acts as a powerful predictor about the capacity of an organization to grow.

At the present, being humble should not be an exclusive attribute to the spiritual leader or an emblematic politician. Humility in the world of business is a powerful value that carries efficiency and merits, among all, if it's accompanied with vision and will. The leaders can amplify the effect of its actions if they provide feedback and favor the autonomy of their followers, even allowing them to make mistakes. To reach the top of the organizational hierarchy, it is necessary to use humility. Once you achieve your desired rank, continuing being humble will make easier the efficiency in results.

The leader that makes the difference is the one that tries to connect with employees and invites them to express, without restrictions, their concerns and judgements. Self-control is one of the keys to a successful life. Many studies have indicated that a constant observation to oneself leads, paradoxically, to a limited self-control. So humility does not benefit only the executives but also the employees. Honesty and humility, as well as the capacity of listening, are predictors of peoples performance at work.

The serving leader is the one that prefers to cheer others up, instead of commanding; he or she offer the employees growth opportunities, oriented in a constant search of other leaders who he or she can delegate assignments and commitments. This kind of leader can reach a strong and generalized consensus, mainly with persuasion, interacting with employees individually and creating a bond that with a certain frequency transcends the workplace.

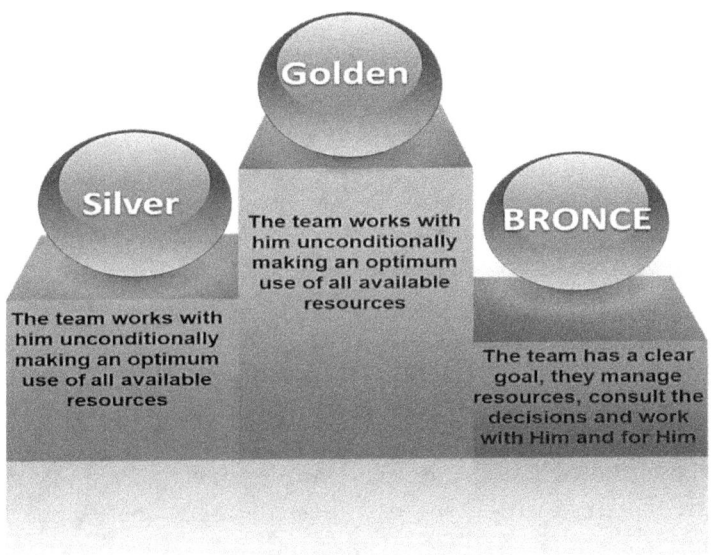

**Leadership Supported in Humility**

**Golden** — The team works with him unconditionally making an optimum use of all available resources

**Silver** — The team works with him unconditionally making an optimum use of all available resources

**BRONCE** — The team has a clear goal, they manage resources, consult the decisions and work with Him and for Him

## Levels of leadership backed in humbleness

### Gold:
- Produces a sustainable greatness, backed in a great dose of personal humbleness. Oriented by the vision of the company, executes actions that allow the company to reach it and overcome it and then to reinvent itself. Listens, identifies trends, processes information, acts with coherence and with a clear vocation for the job, focused on the accomplishment of superior results.

### Silver:
- Generates commitment with the goal of achieving results linked to a clear vision of the organization. Its ethic encourages high performance rules and is focused in actions regulated by humility and the fulfillment of goals.

### Bronze:
- Plans and organizes personal and resources with the objective of achieving predetermined objectives in an efficient way.

The models of leadership that are located outside of the aforementioned categories, indorse their management exercising power and control, worship the leader and not results or what is most convenient to the company or society.

To analyze and know in depth the correct mix between leadership and humility, it is fundamental to check the works of those who have studied the origins of the models of leadership, using history and the data derived from social behavior as support. It is naive to think that answers from the background will arrive by chance, this is the reason why we insist on checking the thesis of great scholars of the subject, such as Samuel Huntington.

A very little group of social scientists have been object of so much controversy as Samuel Phillips Huntington (1927-2008) professor of Political Science in Harvard University and member of the Security Council of the State, during the presidency of Jimmy Carter.

The difficulty to classify S.P. Huntington in a certain ideology, is because the use of scientific methods combined with his natural distrust to leaders and false consensus based in desires more that in viable projects. Both the causes of his impact and the severity of the controversies generated by their proposals are resumed in three main theses:

Rejection to simplifications and his beliefs about continuity to analyze the phenomena of leadership.

- Ease to generate simple and concrete concepts, far away from complexity
- His endeavor to transform political science in an explanatory tool with the capacity to predict the future (analyzing dominating trends and countertrends)

## The political order in societies in a process of change (governability, leadership and humility)

The book *Political Order in Changing Societies* (1968) from the social scientist Samuel Huntington, is a classic that is still alive. In his content it develops the thesis about democracy as an non-viable model of leadership as long as the politicians do not give up the idea of buying the wills of citizens with promises and by trying to make them worship their persona. The creation of democratic governments covered by subsidies and deficit is not sustainable. The Rule of law doesn't have the capacity to provide the citizens with the basic goods for their subsistence, for the contrary it is the institution that in an optimal and fair way facilitates the process so everyone can get a job.

In the context of this work, Huntington develops one of the most influential concepts in Political Sciences in the last 50 years: Governability. The scientist proposes that "the most relevant political difference between countries isn't the way of governing but the grade of government" (S.P. Huntington, 1968).

He affirms that the most dangerous things to democracy are the false promises of equality and equity because they only add the corruption of the poor to the already existent corruption of the rich. By then, the state bureaucracies should not amplify their powers, but to do the opposite: Being humble and limiting themselves to let the things develop in a natural way and this way facilitating the transformation from a traditional society to another one that is modern and democratic.

The proliferation of government leaders and populist companies, backed on corrupt and costly bureaucracies, use resources from the institutions they lead and focus them in assistance that they cash out later with obedience. This way they create cultures of citizens that depend on the business leader or the State. In this scenario, the cult to the personal image is the objective, without caring about the debts of the company or the nation in the future. These were some of the lucid visions of the political scientist that were written 45 years ago.

A country, or company that uses different kinds of leadership to the ones framed into the categories: Gold, Silver and Bronze, put in evidence that humility is not a part of their work culture, or the criterion to achieve superior results. It is inferred that they discard this essential aptitude to increase and enhance conducts. His efforts are localized in the cult to the leaders, however, it doesn't establish commitment with results but with orders; the questioning is understood as high treason and creativity is penalized. In this model of leadership people work just for the leader but not with him. Even though it's hard to imagine, this mode of leadership is still being put to practice from a little family business to a nation's government.

## Individualism and crisis

When a crisis shows up people often get complicated, businessmen often tend to assume two attitudes derived from fear and their own limitations: fatalism or individualism. The fatalism considers that the crisis is national or worldwide; so there's not much he can do to keep his business alive and moves the guilt to those who originated the situation; they created it so they must solve it.

The fatalist stays still, considers himself lost before the fight, the most he can do is hide until the end of the crisis, if it happens. To the fatalist we could ask why others, in the same conditions, move forward? He'll probably excuse himself to justify his inaction. Likewise, it is frequent that the individualist has the 'every man for himself' mentality. He adopts a selfish and anarchist posture. Tends to isolate himself from others arguing that he's not willing to go down with them.

In moments of crisis those who are at the top of companies should apply humbleness with more steadiness, because they need more help, working with their teams and subordinates to move forward, receive thankfully their collaboration and listening to them. In an equal way, sharing the knowledge, keeping alive the solidarity and, mainly, to form work teams that are willing to overcome the adversities. In the book 'The Seven Cultures of Capitalism' (Hampsden-Turner)(1995) it is said that, for the United States, one of the most powerful countries economically, the outstanding traits are: Universalism in the management of businesses and the individualism of those who manage these universal businesses

Universalism and individualism are models that have as a purpose the common work of the individuals, without needing to form communities. The corporative systems are not designed so people detach themselves from their individuality but to make them work together in the most optimal way; thus; they won't be able to achieve important accomplishments staying on their own.

When the organizational climate of companies considers the human as a person, they are not identified by their rank but with relevance. The person isn't isolated from the others, on the contrary, it's bound to them. Only the companies that are composed of people (with character and self destination bonded to others) are capable of forming high performance teams, fortified and with the capacity to deal with complex situations that would be impossible to overcome individually.

## Is selfishness an option?

When we talk about selfishness and generosity in the business world and in our daily lives thinking that man is by nature selfish is a mistake; but a bigger mistake would be to think that the businessmen should be selfish so that he can do well in life. In past times two species with natural trends were distinguished from man. One, in that desire represented the human propensity to acquire the things we lack of; and another, the effusion one, which is related to sharing what we have with others.

For a long time it has been thought that the most powerful trend in men is the desire, while the effusive is like a weak impulse that would come out in rare occasions and in superior people. This belief is inserted and fortified in organizations with frequent failures. Companies require, to their economic success, more humble people, oriented to generosity and not to selfishness. Those who didn't learn to be generous in the family core have a hard time being this way at the company. Among the selfish people it is common to find people with emotional trouble, which can make good money with their work to then lose it in the bills they must pay for their health.

## When should leadership be shared with subordinates?

Many organizational theories have tried to answer this question about the grade in that a manager or director should share the power or authority among their subordinates in the decision-making and the execution of those decisions. One of the most recognized organizational sociologists, Stephen Robbins, from San Diego State University, has numerous arguments to focus this question in the center of the problems of leadership. These arguments allows him to conclude that the most solid type of leadership is the one that backs itself in shared work, where the participation of the members of the team is more active than the figure of the authoritarian leader.

Robbins proposes that the transition people have given to the concept of leadership - being considered as a team - in a whole, it is like we are treating a piece whose parts are not separable, and it is qualified as a different leadership than what we know of. The relevant point of this organizational system is that it funnels the initiative and the sense of responsibility of the members. This system can be called leadership, more appropriately than the one that is attributed as the quality of a person.

The leadership is not the leader, but the organizational system, which allows the members of a team to act better contributing to the fullest of their capacities. Individualities, as a pillar for the results of a company, are a thing of the past, because the power that pretends to increase the growth of itself in a progressive way becomes outrageous and uncontrollable; it forgets that its natural destiny is to be shared by all the collaborators.

Teamwork, in the current moments, is an essential condition to the achievement of a goal. If in a moment of the past "the patriarchs of the company" could drag an organization, today we find that, among the serious and responsible companies, there's a team that's well cohesive in that they have managed to eliminate the excessive personalism of their members and that value constant work, backed in humility.

The models of leadership become in some way behavior models for the leader. Also, they could be defined as the degrees of humility of the leader, if it wasn't because here not only his humility counts, but the capacity of his subordinates. In this models of participation the leader could be defined in the following ways:

- **Autocratic dictator.** The chief solves the problem or takes a decision based on the facts that he knows; everyone does what the boss tells them to.
- **Autocratic.** Collects the information that he wants to listen from his subordinates, and from this he makes decisions. If he succeeds then his call was right, but if he fails he blames the team.
- **Advisory 1.** Shares in an individual way the problem with

relevant subordinates and gets his ideas and suggestions, but the final choice is only his.
- **Advisory 2.** Shares the problem with his subordinates and the team, getting their ideas and suggestions. Then the decision he takes can or cannot reflect the influence of his subordinates.
- **Coach.** Shares the situation with subordinates as a team. Gathers information to make a decision. His ideas as a leader do not have a heavier weight than others.

In this model the influence of the boss is diminishing while the team influence is increasing. This has a direct relation with the humbleness of the leader and, as it was already told, with the capacity of the team members to contribute. This is the general vision of the participation. Therefore, we can conclude that the capacity of a team to contribute is increased in proportion with the capacity that its leader has to put in practice humility.

To make the compounds of a team take decisions without consulting the boss, we need the presence of the three Cs

- Cognizance.
- Communication.
- Cultivacion.

The mutual influence between the leader and his collaborators is enriched by the trust and the participation it generates, focusing the effort on the common goals of the team and the organization. To develop and maintain that culture of work we need leadership healed from arrogance, confident of itself and with a great capacity of putting to practice the competence of humility.

A study published in the year 2011, by the experts Owens Bradley and David Herman, from the Academy of Management Journal, went deeper into the behavior of a humble leader, his contingencies and results. The report concluded that the style of leadership supported in humility, is focused on the outside, promoting the culture of learning in the team. The executives do not realize the tacit distance between the fact of leading from an office distant to the real field of work, so it becomes necessary for them to attach themselves to the processes and collaborators to know in detail every activity and its implications.

Interpersonal relations are the basic cores of a leadership that is humble and centered. The development of relations goes hand to hand with respect, because of that, appearing to be a close boss isn't enough, you need to be close, according to the study.

## How to be a humble boss?

According to Duane in the Diary Digital Management-Issues, Maintaining a humble conduct shouldn't be a complex thing to do for business leaders, just because it's necessary:

- Being close to the members of his team
- Looking after the people in his surroundings.
- Being emotionally sensitive and sincere to the needs of the group
- To be walking among the areas of work (Not being a office boss) talking and exchanging ideas with coworkers (their team)
- Promoting among the members of the organization the freedom of constant learning, experimenting and growing, acknowledging the strengths of employees in charge, besides admitting with honesty that you never know everything and also have several flaws.

To achieve being a humble and close boss should not be a strategy to remain in charge, but a tool that allows the boss to develop his charisma and to differentiate himself from the rest, contributing to strengthen constantly their reputation and professional image.

## Teamwork and humility:

Teamwork is one of the best therapies to reinforce humility and eradicate selfishness, which represents a significant obstacle to personal and professional development. A human being that tries to do everything on his own only limits his own self, his desires of achieving high goals won't ever be reached. Teamwork is necessary to achieve big goals because it motivates, and the people who are involved will give their 100% effort to be the better version of themselves. This goal is accomplished when talents are put together and each one of them contributes from their capabilities. In a real team there are no significant differences that separate the collaborators from the leaders. This principle is based in humility, because the work in which everyone participates is the most suitable habitat to the development of men. In this habitat, leaders dose their influence to make room for the spontaneous work of the collaborators, because when they develop confidence, they manage to convince others and capture their collaboration; it's backed in their ability to exert influence. Because of that when the desire of serving and collaborating with others appears, we begin to put in practice humility making easier the formation and consolidation of future leaders.

According to Peter Drucker, the first lesson that business schools should teach is responsibility, each student must learn to assume their acts and themselves. This action enables it to be transmitted to all the members of the team. This implies that the boss should share the success and assume the failures, in an act of humility that he will exert when it's necessary. Namely, a synthesis between the coordination of the team and his own responsibility must be accomplished. This very important competence should be developed in a team. To achieve it, teams must have a clear vision of the organization as a whole, and the manager should accomplish the following premises:

- Identifying opportunities so that the personnel can develop their capabilities and improve their performance.
- Creating a climate of support reducing the organizational barriers that might come along.
- Motivating the participation of the members to identify the ideas that allow the organization to improve and optimize work processes.

## The cycle of humility

## Domain of the mind and positive thinking.

Our mind is a great mystery. In it are contained the codes of evolution, experiences and conditionings of our state of mind. The mind is an organ of perceptions and actions. It drives the states of mind that have their origin in it. Nonetheless, it isn't common that people exercise to know their mind deeper and practice a control over it, if it's needed or knowing when to think and when to stop doing it.

Frequently we hear that someone suffered a disease because they were predisposed. Also, it can happen that the doctor diagnoses us a predisposition to suffer from a certain condition. But, in reality, what does predisposition mean? How is it related with the mind and humbleness?

Predisposition can be defined as a previous disposition of the state of mind of an individual to a certain end. When a person proposes to carry out a task, they present a certain state of mind that is constructed in their minds and conditions the disposal of himself to the accomplishment of his goals. We can see a clear example of this in sports; before a game, the athlete focuses and reinforces his physical and mental fortitudes so that he can achieve a superior performance. A competitor who is insecure before the match can hardly win because: He's predisposed to failure.

This happens frequently in our daily lives when ego and distrust take over our thoughts. We develop a sensation of being excluded from the background, not because it is really happening but because our mind builds this perception. Also, the lack of humility doesn't allow us to understand that others can be protagonists too, that we're not always right and that in many cases silence is not wasted time.

A personality that is often sad and melancholic will be predisposed to depression. For this people, it is only necessary that something doesn't happen the way they wanted and their behaviors of pessimism, reluctance or sadness instantly appears. Not everything is negative. Likewise, there's a predisposition to positive things. The person who is confident, practical, and well-formed is bound easily with success.

In our minds we build certain predispositions because it hosts the functions of intellect, memory, imagination, attention and consciousness. We are the heirs of the mind we are what we think. To achieve a correct practice of the principle of humility, each of us should be responsible about their minds and start to practice it, enlighten it, calm it and lead it in the right way.

The mind can liberate or imprison. It can make us feel and watch things that aren't really happening. Everything is lived in the stage of the mind. Are we really masters or slaves of it? The mind is developable, improvable and controllable. If the models and reactions of the mind can be modified, so can its habits and tendencies to dispersion. For that, we must follow a mental discipline and carry out a strategy that makes the mind an organ which is subordinated to consciousness. To achieve that we require humility, motivation, effort and discipline.

The development of consciousness and attention is a very powerful element that can only be accomplished through conscious action in our daily lives. We have to be more attentive to have less negative thoughts. When we improve our attention the action is more focused and we can self-regulate our thoughts. Practicing humility and thus being humble consists, in the first place, on a construction of the mind that allows us to identify limitations, with the objective of learning and understanding the reach of possibilities.

For example, at first we assume that we don't know something in order to access new knowledges. If we accept our limitations we'll take consciousness of everything that we have to do or learn. The person who believes that he*she knows everything won't be able to go further. Pride is imposed before humility and produces cocky people and, in the worst of the cases, resentful one.

Being humble isn't a synonym of being weak or naive, but the opposite. Being humble is to have greatness of heart, mind and spirit to understand our surroundings clearly and to contribute with a particular force to make reality seem richer and complete, full of opportunities. In modern day dynamics there are obligations, social pressures, projects to accomplish and people to whom we must answer shortly and not let down. It's obvious that in the middle of so many activities people plunge in their routine where it's complicated to visualize what really brings happiness to the table. Nonetheless, here is where the humbleness begins: acknowledging which are the important things, where family has a main role over the rest of the partial satisfactions or material ones.

## Thinking positive

Each time there's more scientific and experimental evidence about the immense power of thought in our lives, both positively and negatively; to heal and open new paths, or to get sick and to shut down opportunities. Investigators from the Department of Physiology of the Columbia University (USA, Nature, Science. XXIV, 08/23, 2006), using radioactive isotopes as biological markers in human antibodies (proteins and elements of our organism biological defenses) proved that we just need a minute of negative and self-destructive thoughts for human immunological capacity to be modified by six hours.

Dr. Carl Silmonthon, oncology researcher at Harvard University, has clinical evidence and statistics of how pessimistic and defeatist attitudes make cancer cells proliferate and form tumors. In another sense, Dr. Martin Seligman, creator of the concept of Positive Psychology and author of the book Authentic Happiness, proves with solid arguments, backed in plenty scientific investigations, how the optimist and positive people have overcome serious diseases, personal tragedies and conflictive situations, thinking positively when everything fell apart on their surroundings, becoming heroes and saviors of their own lives.

From another perspective, Quantum physics proves to us that we are composed of pure energy (the matter is also condensed energy) and thus are also energy. Thoughts are permanently creating the reality that we live in. Scientists affirm that, thinking of certain issues load the quantum field of the reality we live in, and because of that they can produce phenomena that alter the possibilities. Researchers of subatomic particles know that their thoughts affect on an irremediable way the results of their experiments.

With all this background we must take responsibility of what we think of ourselves, of reality, of others and the future. People are the main characters of what will happen in the future. Every thought, every attitude, emotion and action weave plot of the rest of the life we have to live, meaning we cannot stop planting the harvest we are going to receive.

Each time we are more aware of the relationship between humility and positive thinking, because our aptitude in the face of life plays a fundamental role to build the guideline that allows us to modify negative behaviors in the way that we need to process the things that happen and to apply more constructive strategies. We need to take in consideration these keys to help ourselves rethink feelings, acts and thoughts on our daily basis. Practicing these strategies contributes to taking a weight off our shoulders because we understand that it is impossible to know everything and we learn to ask for help when it is required.

Among the main keys to integrate humility and positive thinking, we have:

- Not developing ideas like: zero sum or everything or nothing. Assuming extreme positions among several subjects is simple, the complex things about this kind of situations is understanding the point of view of others and proposing our own without being offensive. To achieve that we need humility, understanding that when you not transgress values, reality isn't "black or white" or "Right or wrong". When we think in those terms rigidity is increased. There's no place to hues or more wide approaches, the mind develops tendencies to polarize its thoughts and anguishes or exaggerations are generated, in many cases by things that are not happening, and even distant from the reality that can make us set our personal relationships from the perspective of friends or enemies.

- Not generalizing. When a person misses, that doesn't mean this occurs in every case. Conclusions that begin with "always" or "never" usually lead us to exaggerations and to include in failures people that weren't involved.

- Not focusing on a negative perspective. Situations have different points of view. If we choose to highlight the worst things, everything will look bad. For example, giving more importance to criticism than to compliments.

- Highlight the good things that are happening. For some facts we are unaware of, in many opportunities our accomplishments go unnoticed in the routine, without understanding that, if we ignore them we lose the opportunity to appreciate their advantages. Seeing the good things, even in hard moments, is a tool that strengthens us and allows us to reinforce the personal value and self esteem, also it makes us capable of sizing the magnitude of our problems, valuing the personal competences to face it.

- Avoiding predictions and predispositions. Before people or complex situations we issue value judgements, sometimes in our minds, and we anticipate the worst scenarios with their respective conclusions. Thinking that we do not like a person or that something will not go well, impacts the final results. Another very important element is saying no to suppositions when we believe that someone else (friend, couple, partner) thinks or feels a certain way. How do we know it is like that? Validating and asking is always better than supposing.

- Not being victims. Phrases or feelings like: Why always me? Or "I always have bad luck". Why do others have it and I don't? This keeps us away from the responsibility of personal acts and the power we have to make our own decisions.

- Not tagging ourselves. When we make a mistake, not everything that shapes the person deserves to be disqualified. Something similar happens when others make mistakes. It isn't the same thing to say "I did this wrong and I can make it right" that to say "I'm a fool" always having clear that this doesn't imply that we need to hold others accountable for our own mistakes.

- Putting limits to our own responsibilities. If we believe that we are responsible of every problem (a divorce, a son that disapproves, social problems...) we will only feel guilt. In this hidden idea, another more negative and completely set apart from humility: thinking that everything is under the control of one person.

These are some of the guidelines that help us think positive without stopping being realistic and maintaining humbleness; acknowledging the existence of problems that must be faced and overcome. Also, admitting that this forms part of our life dynamics, but knowing that there are solutions to be discovered, strategiesto make us feel better, and amongst all, so we can learn and comprehend that with our way of being and thinking we are shaping the future that we'll live in. The reality is dynamical, and each day is different from the other, many times, when there's no concern about a certain subject that happened, we blind ourselves and we don't see that the reason why we are suffering has already changed.

We cannot think positively when we are prisoners of pride or resentment. Because of that when there are problems and frustrations, we must use humility. In those we must listen, composing our spirit, evaluating the situations and generating positive thoughts. In adversity this isn't easy and it requires consciousness and discipline, but it's necessary to understand this reality because it opens up the way of knowledge and solutions.

## Appreciative inquiry and positive thinking in companies.

The first cases referred to the study about Appreciative inquiry are originated in Case Western University (Ohio) in the decade of the eighties. They were conducted by researcher David Cooperrider and his team; they took as a reference concepts of positive psychology and social constructionism. The proposal of this team is based in that metaphors and language create a narration that has more influence in social structures and organizations.

The Appreciative Inquiry is a collective process in which the members of an organization identify something they do really well with the purpose of making it better and optimizing performance in this matter. This perspective is the opposite to another one more frequent that is centered in correcting the things we're doing poorly.

The Appreciative Inquiry creates opportunities to achieve an outstanding performance from our present strengths. A conjunct vision of what we are doing well generates a collective vision of the future potential of the organization. This shared positive image guides us through the growth and establishes changes sustained in the collective forces, in many cases ignores or underutilized.

The application of this model of thought supposes a deep change in Latin American culture, because it substitutes the model of management that is punitive and condemnatory, focused only on searching and identifying problems, besides chasing guilty people, for the identification of what's functioning well and how we can obtain more from these qualities.

Organizations have a similarity with personality and its leaders' behavior, when in high levels we talk about the bad things and objectives that have not been reached, the message we pass to the collaborators is pessimistic and limits the opportunities of improvement and growth. Those who have the responsibility to guide human teams, can see in the model of Appreciative Inquiry a tool that enables them to augment the satisfaction of the collaborators, and also improving productivity, optimizing the system of communication with different groups of interest, stimulating creativity and aligning their organization with the vision, mission, objectives and strategies.

The egocentric person lives his life thinking that existence limits senses, besides from the mind and intellect. If our ego is big, we identify less with the soul, because the pride is the principle that rules their conduct. Not in vain, big companies like: Cisco, Verizon, Harley-Davidson, Bank of America, John Deere, BBC, British Airways, Avon, Non-profit organizations and communities from Africa, Asia, Europe, North America and South have applied this methodology and succeed, because, as Peter Drucker affirmed "The goal of leadership is to create an alignment between forces so powerful that make the weaknesses irrelevant." (Drucker, 1995).

## Humility in little things:

Humble people are discreet with their successes. Practicing humility is a daily exercise that moves with the responsibility of doing things well, compromising, and doing what's right and necessary with authenticity.

Little things are the ones that weave the actually important acts, those simple codes that matter so much: A smile, a word, a gesture of empathy... codes that aren't bought, but come out from the deepest part of our being; aspects that are installed in memory and generate enjoyment of the little things practicing humility.

Knowing how to listen and understanding silences, being receptive, close and sincere, are characteristics that define humble people. Those that with so much confidence contribute to our development and where we should look true friends. The value of humility doesn't require material objects. The "intangible" dimensions are the ones that really contribute to our wellbeing, real happiness. It's here where the real quality of life is, in simple things.

## Ego management:

From the spiritual approach, ego is considering yourself different and superior to others due to the identification of the physical body. The egocentric person lives his life thinking that existence limits senses, aside from the mind and intellect. If our ego is big, we identify less with the soul, because the pride is the principle that rules our conduct.

## Masks in the sky:

This masks requires flatters, approbation from others, needs to have control of the situation and over people, because in the most deep part of his being there are doubts and fears. The ego believes to be superior to hide the sensation of feeling inferior. The ego is a character in the making. It drives you away from humility and characterizes itself because of its pride, arrogance and excess. Those ways of being shape up their ideal, acting to demonstrate a fake self-esteem that needs to be projected so that nobody sees the insecurities that lay at the bottom of the individual.

## The ego from a psychological perspective:

In simple terms, ego can be defined as an unmeasured pride about oneself, accompanied with thoughts such as: my body and mind, my intellect, my life, my wealth, what I have... among others appreciations. Ego also can be a dislocated consciousness about oneself, loaded with pride, presumption and egoism.

## Ego and humbleness:

A person with an exacerbated ego always talks about what he has and not what he is. He expresses himself with negative words towards others and lives clinging to what he thinks he is and not what really defines him as a human being.

When a person is dominated by their ego, the opinion they have about themselves distorts the true being and gets driven away. Because of that, they're not capable of recognizing themselves. They fool themselves so they do not see reality; they introduce themselves as they would like to be, instead of who they really are. Ego is a social mask that moves away from truth and humility as a value.

## ¿What happens when ego dominates you?

A person with an ego problem has a big flaw; they will not take risks due to their fear of failure, they tend to remain in a comfort zone and routine where they feed their own ego with flattering and acceptation. The known terrain is the habit of their own lives. They don't want to tackle new situations because they fear receiving rejection or critiques. On the opposite side, a humble person is open minded among new knowledges, they have a true self-esteem and they are not afraid of diving into new experiences because disapproval from others do not bother them, they capitalize their mistakes to learn from them without compromising their own personal value.

## What happens if ego is not fed?

When ego isn't fed, the person feels bad, the emotions manifest into negative behaviors, such as shyness, anger and fear. Here they put in evidence their fake mask of confidence, because when the person receives criticism they do not accept them. If the masks falls it is possible that if it isn't obtunded, the person will see that truly, they're not what they believe they are. For the ego, individual identity depends on what others think, when it rules over the life of a human being it weakens him and puts him at the mercy of appearances.

## Being oneself and dominating ego

The ego develops in people who do not accept themselves the way they are, creating an effect of protection amongst supposed attacks. This, instead of calming them down, produces very particular effects that confuse them driving them away from their true being. To control ego we need to feel safe about our personal value, knowing our capabilities and understanding our limitations to improve them, tossing aside the necessity of pretending to be what we are not and enjoying simple things.

It is important to highlight that many of the needs for outside acceptance are not more that illusions created by the ego. To achieve goals we only need to work with others, listening, learning and practicing on a daily basis the competence of humility. Not pretending to be more or believing we are less, because in the end we are all equals.

Humility allows us to accept ourselves and value good moments. The interior essence isn't complex, we must opt for the enjoyment of simple things, appreciating beauty of life and searching for personal satisfactions (practicing hobbies, sports, learning constantly, personal care, spending time with other human beings, loving others and oneself, among other activities.

It is hard to know ourselves, because pride is something that every human being has; it shades up our consciousness and justifies our mistakes. It is usual that, when facing a fact in which our acts might have been negative, our pride refuses to acknowledge that this action was real, and we lead ourselves to believe that we acted wrongly because of others.

Once we get a deep knowledge of our own self is that we achieve the Second Step of Humbleness: Accepting our own reality. Which is normally hard to accept because pride usually shows up when we are exposed to reality, especially when it's ugly or defective. Accepting ourselves isn't the same thing as resigning. If we accept with humbleness a certain flaw, mistake or limitation, we learn to improve and if it is possible to overcome it. We don't walk blindly, but instead focus our energies to achieve something.

The corporate activities are alive and, like personality, the behaviors are the ones who manage it. There are no common models for all the organizations; they will depend on certain needs and moments. Frequently people develop new theories and approaches to human problems in organizations; it is clear that companies ruled by egos are doomed for failure. It becomes necessary to complement professional and personal life, balancing competence with desires of cooperation and putting in practice humility as an essential tool in the construction and consolidation of personal and entrepreneurial leadership

> **Ego drives us away from others, humility brings us closer**

## Eight steps to be more humble

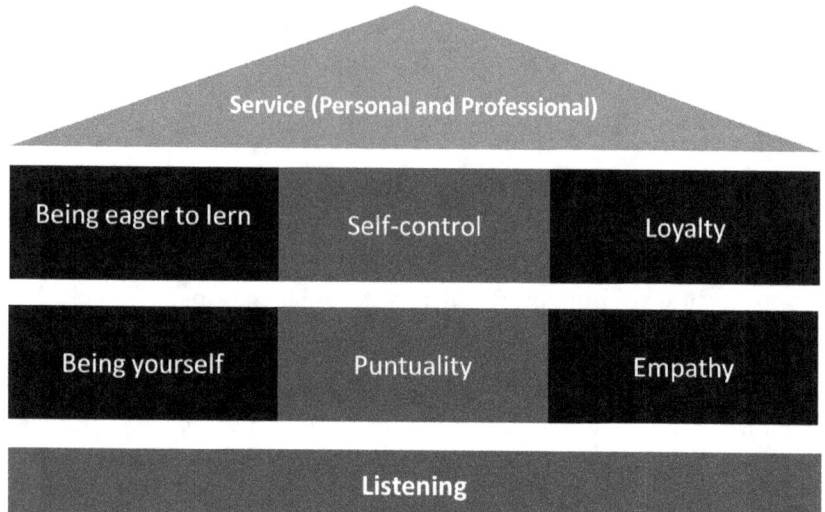

# 4 LISTENING

## Communication and humility in practice

Listening is the route to a more satisfying communication. Leading the attention towards the words of others and searching for the correct perception of the definitions they are transmitting to us. From this point we can extract the message, without judging them previously. In this way we will answer with property when we understand the information provided by the speaker. It is always a challenge, because we stop being the center of our thoughts to dedicate attention to others.

It is symptomatic that values of humility and listening become more evident when a leader is holding a high ranked position of the hierarchic structure, because the path to his promotion has been supported with his capabilities on translating them to the field. This fact is because humble leaders are the ones who benefit the most on organizational cultures where learning, honesty and listening are the main actors.

Listening is a comprehensive process where we not only put attention to the message, but also to the feelings and emotions transmitted by the intermediary. A part of this process is to rethink some ideas or the main concept to test that we have understood the message properly; this feedback is defined as active hearing.

The person who knows how to listen can follow mentally the line of thought of the speaker, select the main ideas of the speech, remember previous ideas and connecting them to others

Through this dynamic we are showing interest and understanding, at the moment of asking for clarifications. The main barriers to achieve an effective hearing are the lack of humility, disproportionate egos and the trend to judge people. These conducts (mistaken) work as perceptive filters that distort the message that is transmitted. This noise that obstructs the communication and effective comprehension, is provoked by self-made ideas, stereotypes about the speaker or the content of his message.

## Elements that limit listening are:

- **Rehearsing.** Thinking about what we are going to say when the speaker finishes
- **Dreaming while we are awake.** Letting our mind wander around.
- **Filtering.** Listening only to one part of the conversation and disregarding the rest.
- **Completing.** Interrupting the speaker to complete the phrase because we think we know what the other person is going to say.
- **Reading the thought.** Trying to guess what the person is saying without even allowing him to explain
- **Interrupting.** Interfering on the speech or the conversation.
- **Reassuring.** Telling the people that everything is fine and ignoring their feelings.

These barriers generate an incomplete hearing, in this case humbleness is needed because it balances everything and allows us to listen to others, putting ourselves in a secondary position, which is an essential condition to achieve active hearing and being better communicators. Before answering to question something, we must argue. When the other person undergoes very strong feelings and wants to pose a certain issue, is when we must put in practice the humility of the active hearing with the purpose of:

- Confirming that we have understood the words and the meaning they have.
- Demonstrating interest.
- Eliminating the "They do not understand" syndrome.
- Encouraging the person so that they explain in depth what they are saying.
- Being able to codify certain significances that are not so evident.

## Keys to achieve active hearing

- Showing understanding and acceptance through our tone of voice, facial expressions, gestures, visual contact and posture.
- Trying to put ourselves in the place of the speaker understanding what he's saying and the feelings he evokes.
- Focusing on what we are saying.
- Maintaining a neutral position
- Not underestimating other people.
- Reflecting our thoughts.
- Not trying to have the spotlight of the conversation: interrupting, giving advice, suggestions or bringing to the exchange similar issues to the ones the speaker is talking about, among other obstacles.
- Encouraging: Developing an interest for the subject that the other person expresses and stimulating them to go on, without showing approval or disapproval.
- Rethinking: Repeating fundamental ideas with our own words to validate that we have heard and understood the message.
- Reflecting: Demonstrating the speaker that you understand how he feels.

Listening carefully is a positive thing for the self-esteem of the person that is speaking; it creates a positive environment for communication, interpersonal relationships and widens directly our vocabulary. It will never be redundant to reinforce that the organizations are communicational networks. Human beings are not only intelligent or reasoning, they also have feelings and emotions; because of that we need to come closer to communication so we can understand relationships with society.

For the human being it isn't enough just to say the things, we need to be heard.

Communication should not be mistaken with direction, but there cannot be a directive action if a true communication is not established properly among bosses, colleagues and subordinates. In leadership the importance not only relapses into talking, but in the act of listening, having the ability of listening a basic compound of the communication. Listening and humility have a great connection; you can't be a great leader without being an excellent listener with a significant dose of humility.

Listening has to do with gestures, which are complements to the message. Because of that we need to take a close look, many times a gesture is capable of transmitting more information than a thousand words. The act of listening not only consists on looking other people in the eyes, but also it demands that we understand how are we being watched.

Listening without humbleness is almost impossible. In case of listening we resume the interest to the speaker; we are interested in what he's saying, the way of looking, the gestures and their posture. Even the person as a whole. When we listen we get the other persons message at its fullest. Also we accept that our own thinking is limited, that the conjunction of different perspectives can provide a bigger picture. It is here where the communion between being humble and listening is located.

Listening means to focus our attention in the person that is speaking, being predisposed to thinking that what he's going to say will be interesting, helpful and true. Besides, that what he's saying is supported in valid reasons, which doesn't imply to accept as a true or as your own everything he says. Listening and accepting are two different actions and should not be confused, we always have the option of not sharing what we hear and to counter their arguments we need to listen closely so we can understand what they're trying to say.

**Listening is:**
- Remaining silent.
- Looking at the eyes.
- Being careful of what we say and feel.
- Giving time and being patient.
- Rethinking the others message to ensure that we have understood it

**Listening isn't:**
- Distracting ourselves while we doing several things at the same time.
- Giving solutions without giving others the chance to figure them out for themselves.

# The defensive aptitude

Not always the communication amongst subordinates and chiefs is pleasant or fluent. Sometimes it is necessary and, convenient to confront situations or subjects that are hard to one another. In such cases, the attitude of listening opposes being on the defensive, which assumes a certain way of arguing that is against the act of listening, because they are acts that are temporarily separated. We should not defend or argue when we are listening. When I listen and I'm quiet, I look at people in the eye, and pay attention to the concepts and feelings, I'm patient, I assume what the other is telling me and repeat it if necessary, with my own words. A good listener can be harsh and direct towards the problematic situation, and soft with the persons involved. It is easier to understand each other referring facts and not value judgements.

## Looking out to learn

The environment is changing, there are things that are happening continuously on our surroundings that offer us knowledge and lessons; we can learn from all (from persons located at the base of the pyramid of an organization and from the highest managerial levels) if we remain vigilant to realize and not judge anybody for their appearance or position. Frequently we get lost in our personal vision and prejudice, wasting the opportunity of getting a general perspective of what's happening, which can be taken advantage of.

If we try hard to be the best we can and have the capacity of being watching out to learn from others, we are ensuring constant learning with real possibilities of application onto practice. Being a permanent observer, with a listening capacity and ease to learn from the environment's wisdom, being quick to identify opportunities or self-improvement, builds the best persona and allows us to understand the organizational processes from the approach of the one executing them, respecting their position and identifying real opportunities to improve them.

## Self-control

Self-control is the capacity of a person to reflect on their desires and actions with solid arguments. When a person lacks self-control, they let their emotions guide them and after that they regret their actions because when we act under the effect of impulses we do not have an objective perspective over the reality.

Self-control is a vital conduct in our professional lives. Dominated by emotions, people can say things that later they regret. Instead, when a person reflects on his or her emotions they can give themselves a time to think about what just happened and speak calmly, controlling what they say.

When someone learns to know himself, they can develop the capacity of predicting some of their usual behaviors. This self-knowledge brings to the table the domain of themselves, being the owner of your acts and words; they have the needed self-control to live a more fulfilling life.

Without self-control we tend to fly off when facing difficult situations and react on an unpredictable way. Self-control grows inside the inner world of each person, avoiding rush, understanding that true happiness depends on a personal decision, that the patience always brings us profit. Thinking before we speak and measuring the consequences of words, as well as understanding the impact of choices will always avoid misunderstandings and add knowledge to the construction of healthy and effective relationships.

Self-control is essential to discipline and the domain of emotions, and opens the gates for reason to be the main criteria in our decision-making. Persons achieve their top when their emotions are kept regulated and under control. Because of this we say that the motivation is individual and intrinsic, because passionate speeches only work to create peaks in emotions and leave restlessness. The most adequate thing is to maintain a gradual process of increasing achievements and emotions. Self-control brings emotional stability and limits our downfalls.

Self-control avoids useless confrontations and losing control of emotions, while self-discipline fortifies judgement and common sense.

How can someone perform to his full potential if their judgement is compromised and his mind is stunned or dominated by shocks and emotions? Self-control keeps him in the present and opens the gate to the future.

# Loyalty

Fulfilling with the things we promise even in changing circumstances. Loyalty is a value, the person who is not able to put it into practice is considered a traitor and as time passes, they'll be left alone. When we are loyal, we accomplish evolving and permanent friendships and relationships, in a sustainable way, in time. Loyalty implies an honest commitment with yourself and others, in good times and bad times, working not only for the wage but because we have a deeper commitment to the company we are working in and society itself.

A trustworthy person must be loyal to those who depend on him/her: family, friends, employees or employer. Loyalty strengthens itself at the moment we learn to watch carefully our attitudes and thoughts. Loyalty develops in our souls, consciousness and has a close bond with other virtues such as friendship, respect responsibility and honesty. When a person is disloyal they manifest it with certain conducts such as:

- Criticizing people, highlighting their flaws, limitations, questioning their jobs, particularly if they're not present.
- Spreading confidence.
- Doing little to no efforts to get a certain job done.
- Promising deadlines for a job and not finishing it.
- Making inadequate comments in public about the appearance of someone else, making them feel bad and diminishing their self-esteem

When business and friendship relations among people are kept in time, they're motivated largely by the use of loyalty as a value and competence. We can work at the top of our capabilities when we are loyal to the team, leaders and the goals they chase. When loyalty is present people achieve an inner peace that allows them to enhance their skills. Loyalty with those we work with is absolutely key to achieve success. It means to maintain the personal respect and knowing how and with who we have alliances; how to relate with team members. Respect fortifies loyalty; it is a unifying force that integrates people to perform as high efficiency teams.

# Punctuality

It is a reality that arriving early to appointments reduces stress, connects in a positive way to the upcoming reunion and makes us gain a good reputation. A competent person has the control of basic aspects of their lives when they fulfill their plans, regardless of the setbacks that might come up. In the contemporary world, when fidelity to commitments is decreasing, those who are capable of accomplishing what they promise earn the respect from their families and people in their surroundings, in case of a first contact they gain the trust of the person with whom they initiated a personal and work relationship.

The most influential management book of al times: The Bible, contains pericopes referred to punctuality where it affirms that: "There is a time for everything, and a season for every activity under the heavens" (Ecclesiastes 3:1). In the context they also mention a "time to plant" and a "time to uproot" (Ecclesiastes 3:2) In the Bible there's also the most relevant and noble reason to be punctual: it is a way to show respect to others and to their valuable time (Philippians 2:3, 4). Those who make others wait are stealing from their time.

Punctuality is the discipline of planning to fulfill our obligations: An appointment at work, a gathering of friends, a work-related commitment, a job that we need to get done. Punctuality is required by human beings because it provides character, order, efficiency and respect for the time of others. When it is applied it promotes the conditions to do other activities, doing the job in an optimal way and building trust.

Tardiness is a bad cover letter that indicates lack of planning for someone's time. When someone stands out for being unpunctual, they soon run out of pretexts and justifications, and this leads to nobody believing what they say.

To be punctual we need to assume with humility that every person, event, reunion, activity or appointment has a certain grade of relevance, and to commit the word and time of others there are enough reasons to count with the presence of the person in the right moment. To put in practice punctuality we need to focus on the activity that we are executing and concentrating not to drift and benefit from the time that we have available.

# I need to be punctual from tomorrow

To internalize this value and human competence, we need to put in practice conducts that produce the right planning of time and punctuality, assuming consciousness that respect for the value of our own time and others time. Among the most relevant reasons we have.

- Analyzing and determining the reasons of the unpunctuality: laziness, irresponsibility, forgetfulness, among other reasons.
- Defining a mechanism to solve the main issue of the tardiness (remind that this requires compromise and discipline) to reduce distractions and breaks throughout the day.
- Drawing up a schedule to establish priorities.
- Using technology configuring a system of "alarms" that help us be more aware of the sense of time and to bring a logical sequence of the activities that we executed and the ones that we haven't done yet.
- Learning to sleep and to wake up early. One of the reasons of unpunctuality is not getting up in time, this leads to an unproductive cycle that translates in going to bed later than when you should, which makes it harder to wake up at the time that you were supposed to. Nothing is more unproductive than opening your eyes in the morning and realizing that it is already late. To avoid this inconvenient it is necessary to learn to respect our own times and the necessities of the body.
- Learning to say no. One of the most frequent causes of unpunctuality is not knowing how to say no. From talking to a colleague when there are other priorities, to attending other activities at work that we shouldn't be doing. Having the humbleness to ask for help, delegating and doing things in the established time is crucial to have a more organized life.

# 5 SERVICE
## Empathy

The quality of service reflects the level of excellence that the person has. The service must be understood as wellbeing for the one who's providing it and for the person that receives it. Serving other differentiates the individuals and puts them in a position to transmit faith, humility, admiration, respect, gratitude, honesty, trust and sincerity. Persons who are capable of serving are always themselves; they don't feel the need to replicate or compare themselves with others, removing the weight from appearances and spending their time in the joy of helping. The one who develops the vocation to serve as a conduct in their lives, always opens the doors to exchanging and receiving the positive things in life, answering to the eternal question: Serving or not serving?

For the companies, service should not be a trend in a world where the commercial offer is increasingly bigger. The service constitutes a differentiating factor for the company to consolidate and develop their position in the market. Even though service and client are bond together and cannot be separated, we must be clear that service isn't a recipe and that we can't simple decree it; service must be a much more real intention associated with a personal habit, a virtue that is exerted in the inner self and ends up generating what is known as vocational service. The service is the disposal that allows you to be aware of the necessities of others, and to satisfy them as far as possible, abandoning ego and practicing humility

A conduct that is associated with service is empathy. Empathy defines itself as the action of understanding the situation of someone else to feel the same things that the other person is feeling.

"Thinking as a client". Normally, in companies it is accustomed to do the work without thinking that it depends on the work of others. Detecting the needs of other people is an achievement itself, but it isn't enough if these needs aren't covered. One of the main factors of management is to pay attention to the people that conform the work team, with the goal ensuring that they have everything they need to get the job done, which has a direct relation with service and empathy.

Service removes the meanness from the individual thoughts of each person and makes them think about others, bringing as a consequence to experience the joy of feeling useful. In companies where the main product is their service, quality can't be measured in a mathematical way and it will depend, almost entirely on the perception of the client; this is why and effective interaction between the client and the company becomes more necessary than ever.

## How to achieve an exceptional service at companies

Quality of there are many practices that could be performed, and the focus of these is customer service and the improvement of the clients perception regarding the service.

- **The strategy.** Establishing in the strategic plan of the company the aspects of the service that they'll provide to differentiate and comprehend the needs of their clients.
- **Sharing the success.** The victories belong to the team and the defeats are taken by the leader
- A leader who is not capable to share the success will lose quickly the respect of his collaborators, building a barrier

between the motivation of his personnel and them making efforts to make the organization successful.

- **Representing the brand of the company.** The leader must update constantly their profiles of social network to ensure that they reflect on a positive way the business or the company they represent.

- **Having high standards.** Determining frequently and exactly the needs of their actual and potential clients to adjust the quality of the service according to their needs.

- **Tracking the performance.** Measuring the performance of the collaborators to enforce behaviors associated to service and applying certain actions to improve them when they lay below the established standard.

- **Customer service.** Regardless of the size and position of leadership, companies should have the humbleness to listen to the client and look out for trends in the market, because they'll allow them to develop new products to attend changing necessities and to increase their competitiveness. Also, paying a lot of attention to the complaints and suggestions of the clients.

- **Satisfaction of the collaborators.** The collaborators are those who represent the company, which should have a positive relationship with them, providing an adequate physical and cultural environment for work. Rewarding contributions and conducts that are oriented to improve the quality of the service it provides.

The value of the client is the axis of essential changes in the corporate dynamics in the next years. Because of the rising competence, the offered products are each time more similar and the clients do not grow at the same time than the offer. Thus, it becomes essential that the companies transform so they can stand out from others, the factor with more odds to guarantee that positioning is service.

The demands of the clients are growing exponentially because they know how much they are worth; they have had experiences that led them to accept and to reject companies that they were clients from, because there are not many cautious markets left, everything that is done is public. Those companies that have no value for the client which do not put the client's needs first, those companies that are only interested in their money, will not have another option but to change and to do that they must wake up and smell the coffee and put themselves at the same level as the clients, coming closer to them, humanizing themselves, empathizing. In a nutshell, they need to become more humble. Humbleness in a long term creates sustainable relationship between clients, companies and brands.

## Pride vs. Humility

Too much power is a synonym of pride, and it is exercised, in occasion, by people who manage from pride, with the argument of enforcing the rules. If we exchange meetings with leaders with the power to make important decisions in an organization it is easy to identify the type of executive they are by their attitudes and conducts. Some of the most frequent are:

- Boasting: The capacity of praising themselves to highlight their superiority and good deeds, without emphasizing the talent of others.
- The widened ego: Positioning themselves in a superior spot to others talking always about what they have and not what they are; showing in their appearance a luxury that overcomes what his own economical possibilities allow.
- Haughtiness: Becomes evident in the way he treats his collaborators, speaking to them on a stubborn way, with a despicable tone and looking at them with an air of superiority.
- Ambition: The desire of highlighting ranks or positions, considering the benefits and not the responsibilities.

- Inadequate use of language: using a vulgar language to emphasize their points of view.
- Hypocrisy: Simulating virtues to cover their own defects and apparent values and competences they do not have.
- Presumption: Trusting themselves too much and believing they are capable of doing every function better than others, even assignments that exceed their knowledges or capabilities.

The core against pride is humility. Being humble with our family, friends, collaborators, bosses and to every being that we have contact with. Humility ennobles us, it's never bad.

## The company, as a social and economic entity has four purposes:

- Generating wealth or added value
- Serving the community where they develop their activity.
- Developing the collaborators that conform it.
- Being sustainable in time.

The accomplishment of the organizational objectives is related to the social responsibility of the company. You can't be fulfilled while you are socially irresponsible. To achieve our organizational goals, it is crucial that the leaders leave their personal interests aside and begin getting interested on the society they live with. The person who only attends the development of their personal capabilities isn't humble, because they don't care about their surroundings and the persons around them. The attentive and cheering attitudes are compounds of humility and impact in a direct way the growing and development of the collaborators according to their capabilities.

The first goal of a company is to create wealth or added value. This might seem opposed to the spirit of self-serving of the human being and to humility. This clarifies itself when the creation of wealth isn't only pursued to benefit shareholders, managers or directives, but to benefit the community it serves, the workers and future generations. If wealth is handled on a discretional way, it is used with humbleness and allows the fulfillment of other goals of the company, they empower and allow that thing that was born as just an idea to consolidate itself, growing and being sustainable in time.

## Trust

In the world of businesses it is avoided to use terms such as trust and humility, but those who carry out commercial activities know by experience that, without trust, it is impossible to achieve great results; this is why we say it is a value and competence that holds the relationships of the merchant world. A trader who doesn't respect his own words creates distrust, not in his profession, but in his person, limiting his actions because nobody wants to do business with untrustworthy people.

Francis Fukuyama, in his work "Trust", qualifies trust as the most valuable social capital, comparable to monetary capital. According to Fukuyama, social capital can be defined as:

...The capacity of people to work together in groups and common associations, depending on the grade in that a community shares rules and values, and subordinates individual interests to the ones of sets of people.

The leader must not focus exclusively on his technical knowledges and sitting waiting for answers from his collaborators, but rather their activity should be always focused on the wellbeing of others. Leaders have a social responsibility. There's nothing more harmful and conceptualizing leaders as a tool of management.

Exerting personal and business leadership, among all, is humility and service. Understanding the needs of others before the preoccupation to be a figure. The leader must identify himself with the task and the values of the team because it creates confidence in his direction to allow others to fulfill adequately their functions. We do not have to forget that more than the development of the person, in any human team, the one who has the most responsibility is the leader. There is no leadership if there aren't any people to lead. Being a leader has no sense when there are no people and corporative objectives to serve.

The leader must be one with the organization, on a way that his role doesn't stay on the margin of a certain work team. Modeling others is a job that compromises the directives, who, thanks to their position in the organizational structure, have an amplified microphone to project their ideas, They also have the special personal responsibility over their collaborators, which allows them to defend their rights, even before their own. Leadership is always referred to conjunct efficiency, searching for the improvement of the organization as a whole. If a leader only searches for the perfection of an administrative system, they leave aside the people, the company and forget that no important objective is achieved without the participation of a human team. The key is to realize that humility prepares the growing of the collaborators so that they show their qualities, and in that way, facilitate the alignment of personal objectives with organizational ones.

## Can a good professional be a bad person?

Many would answer yes without thinking about it too much. However, Howard Gardner, doesn't think like that. The thinker, investigator, psychologist and professor of the University of Harvard, who has been an outstanding individual in the field of science because of his contributions about the analysis of the human cognitive capacity, among these the theory of multiple intelligences, has wondered:

"Why did people that were considered winners and prominent in politics, finances, sciences, medicine or other fields did negative things for their surroundings and themselves?".

## Ethics and the good professional

As we have said, Gardner wondered about the ethics of intelligence. Is it true that those people who we consider winners are also amazing on their human aspect? Can you really be good at any profession being a bad person?

To answer this complex question, even though at first sight this is pretty obvious, Howard Gardner began an experiment that was known as the Goodwork Project, over whose methodology interviewed over 1,200 people. It was at that point when the amazing results came. Actually a bad person is never a good professional. In fact, although they might have great technical skills, they will never achieve excellence in their field of work and personal lives.

## The best professionals

Once the experiment was done and the results were analyzed, Howard Gardner proposes that every good professional should be ECE. What do those letters mean? It means that an individual who aspires to the highest of performances has to show excellence, commitment and ethics. In any case, many will think that this isn't true. That every bad person can be great at their fields. However, Gardner stipulates that this kind of profile only looks for the satisfaction of their ego and ambition, leaving aside the objectives that chase common benefits. In this case we can be technically really good at performing, but we'll never be able to achieve excellence, because to do that we need to put ethics in practice.

Howard defends ethics and social commitment as unavoidable values to achieve a high performance and professional excellence. Meanwhile, even though we achieve some level of wealth and having a lot of money, we'll never put in practice our whole potential.

## The inertial professional and the transactional student

Another figure that is extracted from Howard Gardner studies is the inertial professional. Those who surrender to social pressure and accept to study and to work because it is what their surroundings demand, but they don't have the interest of developing or putting in practice their potential. Another figure is the transactional student; this allows to analyze young people that study only to get a degree which allows them to access a certain job position to get their salary. This kind of people visualize work life as a sacrifice, something that they must go through to get resources and do not expect to get from their profession enjoyment or satisfaction.

## The happiness of the professional

Talking about happiness at the workplace in today's world isn't ethereal or intangible. Diverse studies have shown that it constitutes an essential factor in the formation of the culture of organizations and has a strategic influence in the development of their proposal of value. We spend more time at work than in anything else in adulthood, so we must seek happiness and labor completeness, supported in the premise that establishes:

**If you love what you do, you have better odds to be happy in your personal life and to live at the fullest**

The objective of every high performance professional is putting in practice his potential through the development of his capabilities, not suffering from vocation crisis and continuously reinventing himself to contribute and improve processes in his daily work. The bad persons or inertial and transactional subjects have serious trouble throughout their lives.

To fix this situation, Gardner proposes to complement the technical study with the learning of humanistic knowledge, such as philosophy, literature, or history of thinking; this way we don't get lost on a few things of the perspective of who we are. We can also avoid over dimensioning the sensation of control that fortifies technological studies.

> **We can't be better managers than people. To be humble: "We need a lot of greatness".**

The renowned Argentinian writer, Ernesto Sábato, when referring to the value of humility, said: "We need a lot of greatness to be humble". Nothing more despicable than arrogance from those who want to have it all, but lack humility of heart to recognize the necessity of asking for help, such as the opportunity to learn from everyone, a person who can't listen to others and offer them help can't be great.

The French writer Anatole Thibault France, in his work 'The Gods are Atheist', affirms "not being ever humble with the arrogant, nor arrogant with the humble." (France, 2010). There are people that, when they achieve holdings, they can even repudiate their own family. "they're full of themselves" and, despite climbing socially (in many cases with doubtful legitimacy) then they fall on a resounding way, victims of pride and vanity. Pride is the flaw of those who only think in their benefits. They don't care about the evil created by their actions. Sharing experiences and knowledge is proper of beings touched by the greatness of humbleness.

A person who does not act with humbleness transforms into an arrogant, distant and despot human being, losing this way their quality of such. Those who live with humility in the family, communities and companies, put in practice a conduct that allows them to focus on their goals achieving them without sacrificing principles or values; they do not compare themselves to others and compete with themselves to be better each day.

# 6. Questionnaire of Humbleness

The pace of life in today's modern world is intense, full of activities and routines and because people have less opportunities to reserve their time, making diagnoses of their behaviors and the impact that these conducts have on their daily basis, achievements and society. A person isn't humble because he says so or because he thinks he is. A person is humble when he is coherent in thinking and action, and when he translates what he preaches into frequent and measurable behaviors.

Down below we introduce a questionnaire that allows you to determine your disposal to put in practice the value and competence of humility. The objective is that you put the answer that best suits your reality or situations as they really happen, not as you would like them to be. It is necessary to remember that the key point is understanding that being humble is a culture of life.

The idea is that your answers act as a diagnosis of the current situation and, thus, provide a map of future actions that are oriented to the search of incorporating, fortifying and reinforcing the presence of humility as a value and competence in your personal and work lives.

1. Do you apologize when you make a mistake?
   a) Never
   b) Sometimes
   c) Very often

2. Do you follow the advices of more experienced people?
   a) Never
   b) Sometimes
   c) Very often

3. Do you consider that if you know a lot about a subject you can't learn more about it?
   a) Never
   b) Sometimes
   c) Very often

4. Do you pay attention to what others think of you?
   a) Never
   b) Sometimes
   c) Very often

5. Do you consider yourself superior to others on an intellectual or economical basis?
   a) Never
   b) Sometimes
   c) Very often

6. When you exchange opinions, do you expose your arguments calmly?
   a) Never
   b) Sometimes
   c) Very often

7. Are you annoyed when someone points out that you did something wrong?
   a) Never
   b) Sometimes
   c) Very often

8. Do brands and other materialistic symbols are influential factors on you to choose your friends?
   a) Never
   b) Sometimes
   c) Very often

9. Do you insist frequently on being right about a certain subject?
   a) Never
   b) Sometimes
   c) Very often

10. Is it hard for you to admit that someone that does not think like you can be right and you can be wrong?
    a) Never
    b) Sometimes
    c) Very often

11. Do you compare yourself to friends or others?
    a) Never
    b) Sometimes
    c) Very often

12. Does asking for help make you in any way uncomfortable?
    a) Never
    b) Sometimes
    c) Very often

13. Do you lie in certain opportunities to give others a good image of yourself?
    a) Never
    b) Sometimes
    c) Very often

14. Do you insist on others' mistakes?
    a) Never
    b) Sometimes
    c) Very often

15. Do you feel that your thoughts have a negative approach?
    a) Never
    b) Sometimes
    c) Very often

16. In a conversation, if you don't talk, do you feel ignored?
    a) Never
    b) Sometimes
    c) Very often

17. Do you believe that people is against you?
    a) Never
    b) Sometimes
    c) Very often

18. When you share leadership do you feel scared?
    a) Never
    b) Sometimes
    c) Very often

19. Do you speak frequently about what you have?
    a) Never

b) Sometimes
   c) Very often

20. Do you like people referring to you after your tittle (academic degree, such as: PhD)?
   a) Never
   b) Sometimes
   c) Very often

## Correction table

Most of the questions answered A (never). It's a person that internalizes humbleness and puts it in practice often. Is vigilant to learn from others and takes care of issuing value judgments, which gives him the flexibility to acknowledge several ways of thinking, highlight their maturity and does not allow influences from elements with whom they don't agree with. Likewise, they try to develop the trust of the ones who commonly don't have the opportunity to share their views with others and they also share their own knowledge with others.

Most of the questions answered B (Sometimes). They have certain fears, and haven't questioned this vision on behalf of others knowledge. There is fear on recognizing that they aren't as prepared as they think and that they can keep learning. The mistake isn't ignoring things, but not trying to learn and discovering them. Not all of the learnings are endorsed by a college degree, and neither by appearances. Allow yourself the opportunity to have open sense to receive the formation and the knowledge that you can get.

Most of the questions answered C (Always) They must work on the control of ego and pride. They are individualistic beings and because of that they reject on the act the opportunity of learning from whom, on their perspective, do not have the knowledge or social level that you require. You must deprive your life from prejudices and stereotypes and you'll be surprised with the amount of doors that will open.

# Epilogue

## Humility

*Facundo Cabral*

Learn from the water because the water is humble and generous with anybody, learn from the water that takes the shape of what it wraps up: in the sea it is wide, narrow and fast in the river, tight in the cup, nonetheless, still soft, carves the thick rock.

Learn from the water that because of its gracefulness it strains among your finger, as gracious as the wheat spike that submits to the desires of the wind and bends itself until they touch the earth soil with its head, but past the wind the wheat spike recovers it's vertical posture, while the oak, that is harsh by nature and does not bend to the wind, is broken by it.

Be soft as the water so that the lord can move you graciously in the fulfilling of your destiny, and you'll be eternal like him, because only the person who lets other transcend them by the transcendental will transcend.

---

**Only when we are great in humility we are closer to the big things...**

*Facundo Cabral*

e.

# BIBLIOGRAPHY

Ackoff, Russell (1990). Planificación de la empresa del futuro. México. Limusa.
Cardona, Pablo (2000). Liderazgo relacional. Documento de investigación No 412. Universidad de Navarra. Barcelona, España. IESE.
Chinchilla, Nuria (2002). Distintos enfoques para la dirección de fenómenos en la organización. En Juan Antonio Pérez López et. al. Paradigmas del liderazgo (p. 7). Madrid. McGrawHill.
Drucker, Peter (1995). Managing in the Next Society. New York, USA. Griffin.
(2002). Son personas. México. Expansión.
France, Anatole (2010). Los dioses tienen Sed. Barcelona, España. Barril & Barral.
Gaos, José (1992). Del hombre. México. Universidad Nacional Autónoma de México.
Goleman, Daniel. Boyatzis, Richard. McKee, Annie. El líder resonante crea más (2002). Barcelona, España. Plaza y Janés.
Greenleaf, R. K (1970). The servant as a leader. Indianapolis, USA. The Greenleaf center.
Hampden Turner, Charles, y Trompenaars, Alfons (1995). Las siete culturas del capitalismo. Buenos Aires, Argentina. Editorial. Vergara.
Huntington, Samuel (1968). Orden Político en las Sociedades de cambio (en español). Barcelona, España. Paidos Ibérica.
Kottler, P. John (1990). What Leaders Really Do. A Force for Change; How Leadership (Review, Mayo-Junio). Harvard, USA. Harvard Business.

Llano Cifuentes, Carlos (1979). Análisis de la acción directiva. México DF. México. Limusa.

(1995). La creación del empleo. México DF. México, Panorama.

(2000). La amistad en la empresa. México DF. México. Fondo de Cultura Económica.

Llano, Cifuentes Carlos (2004 – 2007). Actividad Dimensión externa Dimensión interna. Revista Empresa y Humanismo. Edited by Foxit PDF Editor.

(2004 – 2007). Diagnóstico Objetividad Humildad.

(2004 – 2007). Decisión Magnanimidad Audacia.

(2004 – 2007). Mando confianza constancia.

(2004 – 2007). Lealtad Autodominio.

(2004 – 2007). Fortaleza.

(2004 – 2007). Caracterología del directivo al inicio del siglo XXI.

(2004). Dilemas éticos.

(2004 – 2007). Falacias y ámbitos. La sinergia del trabajo en equipo.

(1996-1). Función, plan y proyecto. Tópicos 10, 25-59

Maslow, Abraham (1954). Motivation and Personality. New York, USA. Harper and Row.

Packard, David (1995). The HP Way. How Bill Hewlett and I Built Our Company. New York, USA. Harper Bussines.

Pfeffer, J. J (1998). The human equation. Boston, USA. Harvard Business School Press.

Robbins, Stephen P. Comportamiento organizacional. México. Prentice-Hall Hispanoamericana.

Rodríguez Porras, José María (2001). Comunicación interpersonal y la empresa. En Juan Antonio Pérez López et al. Paradigmas del liderazgo (pp. 59 y ss). Madrid. McGraw-Hill.

Seligman, Martin E.P (2002). Authentic Happiness: Using the New Positive Psychology to Realize Your Potential for Lasting Fulfillment. New York, NY. Free Press.

Servitje, Lorenzo (2003). El lado humano de la empresa. México. Expo Management 4-VI.

Schein, Edgar (1980) Organizational Psychology. Massachusetts, USA. Prentice Hall.

Spencer, L.M. & Spencer, S.M (1993). Diccionario de competencias de Spencer & Spencer, traducido al español. New York, USA. John Wiley and Sons.

Trout, Jack (1999). The Power of Simplicity. Ontario, Canada. Markham.

# Contents

Introduction ..................................................................................... i

Preface ........................................................................................... 1

1. Humility ................................................................................... 5

    Meaning of humility ................................................................ 5

    The concept of humility .......................................................... 6

    Humility as a value ................................................................. 8

    Humility as a competence ..................................................... 9

    ¿How do you put in practice the competence of humility? ..... 9

    ¿What is a competence at work? ........................................ 11

    Development of the competency model ............................. 11

    Types of competences ......................................................... 12

    How can we incorporate humility to the business model of competences ...................................................................... 13

    What are the conducts associated with humbleness? ....... 13

    Who's the responsible of putting humility into practice? .... 14

    Humility and businesses ..................................................... 15

    How did he do it? ................................................................. 18

2. BUSINESS CASES ..................................................................19

    Humility makes you grow: ..................................................19

    Johnson & Johnson and Tylenol .........................................19

    What happens when a company loses its humbleness? ........19

    The questions arise .............................................................21

3. LEADERSHIP AND HUMILITY ...............................................27

    Should a businessman or a politician be humble? ..............27

    Levels of leadership backed in humbleness .........................30

    The political order in societies in a process of change (governability, leadership and humility) .....................................................31

    Individualism and crisis .....................................................32

    Is selfishness an option? .....................................................34

    When should leadership be shared with subordinates? ......34

    How to be a humble boss? ..................................................37

    Teamwork and humility: ....................................................37

    The cycle of humility .........................................................39

    Domain of the mind and positive thinking. ........................40

    Thinking positive ...............................................................42

    Appreciative inquiry and positive thinking in companies ....46

    Humility in little things: ....................................................47

    Ego management: ..............................................................48

    Masks in the sky: ...............................................................48

The ego from a psychological perspective: ........................................... 48

Ego and humbleness: .................................................................. 49

¿What happens when ego dominates you? ........................................ 49

What happens if ego is not fed? ................................................... 49

Being oneself and dominating ego ................................................ 50

Eight steps to be more humble .................................................... 52

## 4 LISTENING ............................................................................ 53

Elements that limit listening are: ................................................. 54

Keys to achieve active hearing ..................................................... 55

The defensive aptitude .............................................................. 57

Self-control ............................................................................ 58

Loyalty ................................................................................. 59

I need to be punctual from tomorrow ........................................... 62

## 5 SERVICE ............................................................................... 63

Empathy ............................................................................... 63

How to achieve an exceptional service at companies ........................ 64

Pride vs. Humility ................................................................... 66

The company, as a social and economic entity has four purposes: ........ 67

Trust .................................................................................... 68

Can a good professional be a bad person? ..................................... 69

Ethics and the good professional ................................................. 70

The best professionals ....................................................................... 70

The inertial professional and the transactional student ......................... 71

The happiness of the professional ......................................................... 71

6. QUESTIONNAIRE OF HUMBLENESS ....................................................... 73

Correction table .................................................................... 78

EPILOGUE ................................................................................................ 79

BIBLIOGRAPHY ........................................................................................ 81

About The Author

# HILDERMARO INFANTE

General advisor, speaker, professor, writer and motivator of professional sports teams. His experience goes beyond 25 years, holding direction positions in leading companies in the Retail, Mass Consumption and Services.

Director of H. Infante & Asociados (www.hinfante.com), consulting company dedicated to grasping and creating value for its customers, in the areas of Strategic Planning, Procedure Analysis, Key Value of Retail Sector, Work Happiness, Organizational Culture, Value, Competency-Based Management, Development of High Performance teams, among others. As an advisor he has executed projects in Colombia, Equador, Venezuela and Central America.

Graduated from INCAE Business School of Costa Rica, Number 1

Business School of Latin America, Designated as Valedictorian. MBA in Management of Human Resources (UCV) (Venezuela), Bachelor in Commercial Administration (Universidad Simón Rodríguez) (Venezuela). Postgraduate Professor in the Universidad Metropolitana of Caracas, where he also coordinates the Diplomas. He has dictated conferences in Central America, Colombia, Venezuela and Equador, for his audiences of up to 600 participants. His first book "Pyramid of Work Happiness", is sold in Colombia, Venezuela and Central America and his articles have been published in journals in Venezuela, Central America and the United States.

www.ingramcontent.com/pod-product-compliance
Lightning Source LLC
Chambersburg PA
CBHW052332220526
45472CB00001B/383